Spirituality in a Mixed-Up Age

by H. Mark Abbott

SPIRITUALITY IN A MIXED-UP AGE
H. Mark Abbott

All rights reserved. No part of this publication may be translated, reproduced or transmitted in any form or by any means electronic or mechanical, including photo copy, recording or any information storage retrieval system without written permission from the publisher.

All scripture quotations, unless otherwise indicated, are taken from the HOLY BIBLE, NEW INTERNATIONAL VERSION®. NIV®. © 1973, 1978, 1984 by International Bible Society. Used by permission of Zondervan Publishing House. All rights reserved.

ISBN 0-89367-208-4

© 1997
Light and Life Communications
Indianapolis, IN 46253-5002
Printed in the U.S.A.

Contents

What Does Spirituality Really Mean?
1 Hot, Hip and Half True 9
2 Something God Does 17

Spirituality and Real People
3 Abraham: Yes to God's Call 27
4 Jacob: Wrestling with God 37
5 Moses: Face-to-Face with God 41
6 Joseph: Living Our Dreams 51

Spirituality and the Growing Christian (Meditations on Ephesians)
7 Saying Yes to God 57
8 Living in Community 63
9 Indwelt by God 71
10 Integrating Faith in Life 77
11 Using God's Weapons 85

Spirituality and the Holy Spirit (Meditations on Romans 8)
12 No Condemnation 93
13 Belonging 101
14 Help for Hang-ups 109
15 Good From Everything 115
16 Spiritual Music 121

Spirituality — The Difference it Makes
17 Stories and Spirituality 131

| 18 | Roots and Renewal – Transformation | 137 |
| 19 | Taste and See – Thanksgiving | 143 |

Spirituality — Living Between the Already and the Not Yet
20	Advent: Promises and Hope	149
21	Why a Baby?	155
22	Promises Fulfilled	161

Spirituality — From the Depths to the Heights
23	The Cross: A Sob and a Song	169
24	Easter: A Time to Laugh	177
25	Pentecost: From Bones to Body	185

Spirituality and Stewardship
26	Creation Stewardship	191
27	Exodus Stewardship	199
	Endnotes	207

Preface
Making Sense of Spirituality

I live in a part of the country characterized by offbeat spirituality. The Northwest, particularly the Puget Sound region, is a Mecca for the New Age movement, sometimes pseudo-Christian, but actually warmed-over Hinduism. It is fundamentally pantheistic, clearly unbiblical, even when it uses Scripture.

This area is home to ideas of spirituality our forebears certainly wouldn't have recognized as such. The religiously and morally tolerant atmosphere invites all to practice what they see fit as long as it doesn't infringe on other people or isn't imposed upon anyone else. "Truth for you and truth for me," is a major theme.

What we experience in Seattle, however, is merely the prevailing climate of our country enlarged and amplified. Everywhere in America these days people are caught in the ferment of what it means to be spiritual. The word "spiritual" has become so widely and loosely used that it's hard to know what is meant.

In this context, I decided to preach for a year on "Making Sense of Spirituality." Responses by people in the congregation have prodded me to offer this material to a wider audience in a somewhat different format.

5

Spirituality in a Mixed-Up Age

My thanks to the wonderful people of the church I serve for their encouragement to write and their continuing stimulus to the best I can do in preaching. My thanks to my wife, Mary Ann. It is in the context of our more than 30 years of life together that my spirituality and ideas about it have been worked and lived out with varying degrees of consistency.

Thanks to Shannon Havener, secretary-receptionist in our church office, who helped me with computer formatting, commas and my creative spelling. Thanks to the group of men, with whom I meet weekly, all of whom are authors or would-be authors. Our conversation and prayer together has nourished my life and thought immensely.

My thanks to authors Eugene Peterson and Henri Nouwen. As a conscientious pastor, I have often fled to their books for refuge and encouragement from the pressure-filled writings of those who would tell me how to do it in the pastorate. Peterson and Nouwen remind me again and again that it is more important who I am than what I do.

An authentic Christian spirituality is something which grows and develops through the changing seasons of one's life. Though much of such spirituality remains constant, its tone and emphasis often vary with life situations. How God's Spirit works with me is not exactly the same now as it was 10 years ago. I expect it is not precisely now what it will be 10 years in the future.

I am excited to learn and grow, continually receptive to what God wants to make of me and do through me. It is with this sense of being in process that I offer these reflections on Christian spirituality.

H. Mark Abbott

What Does Spirituality Really Mean?

1
Hot, Hip and Half True

Sitting with a bright young couple planning to be married, I was asking them why they wanted to do this radical thing. Both were from Christian backgrounds but had gone through varying degrees of rebellion against their heritage and were not now active in the life of the church. As they described to me why it was they found each other attractive, he said, "She's such a spiritual person." Later, they described the faith and relationship with God they found comfortable at this stage in their lives. "We're into 'creation spirituality,'" they said.

Spirituality in Contemporary America is Hot!

Words of spirituality are frequently used. But what do they mean? It's not easy to make sense of spirituality in the present context.

According to one observer, spirituality today is "out of the closet and within arm's reach at the checkout aisle, along with batteries, toothpaste and the *National Enquirer*."

Browsing "The Companion Line" section of our newspaper, I came across this ad, "Spiritual outlook who likes to have lots of fun." The "come-on" continued: "Petite SWF 48, but looks 38. Nonsmoker or drinker and would prefer the same. Seeking honest, down to earth and spiritual male ..."

When O.J. Simpson's older children were being inter-

Spirituality in a Mixed-Up Age

viewed by Katie Couric during the early weeks of his imprisonment, she asked whether his ordeal had made their father more religious. "More spiritual," was the son's reply.

"Spiritual brunches making the scene in L.A." was a recent headline, describing the resurgence of the Sunday brunch in the Los Angeles area. Added now to the brunch is gospel music. "Praise the Lord and bring on the calories!" the article began. Observed one promoter of this substitute for church, "It's a great way for people who should go to church, but don't."

Not long ago, best-selling author Scott Peck sponsored a $10,000-a-foursome golf tournament to promote, according to him, spirituality, golf and the fine art of business management.

Spirituality today is the "in" thing among beautiful people, socially, if not politically correct. However, the kind of spirituality popular today would not have been understood or approved of by our grandparents.

Spirituality Today is Not What It Used to Be

When I first became a pastor in 1968, being a spiritual person meant being profoundly religious, deeply devoted to God and the church and committed to spiritual disciplines such as prayer, Bible reading and fasting. It meant being at church every time the doors were opened, witnessing for Christ, and maybe volunteering for pastoral ministry or for missionary service.

Sometimes, the spirituality of a generation ago was linked with legalism. It came to mean "Do this, but not that, and you will be a spiritual person." It sometimes entailed lists of written and/or unwritten rules, understood to safeguard the spirituality of the faithful, if not actually producing it.

But spirituality in the '90s isn't necessarily Christian. It may, in fact, be what some are calling "neopagan." Citing his dissatisfaction with a November 1994 *Newsweek* feature on

Hot, Hip and Half True

spirituality, Charles Colson wrote: "The reader was left to conclude that enlightened spirituality in America is confined to New Age neopaganism."[1]

The headline of a *USA Today* cover story on Buddhism among today's Americans announced, "More drawn to the no-frills spirituality." The article estimated that there are 800,000 Buddhists in the United States. Among them are such stars as Chicago Bulls' Phil Jackson, Tina Turner, Courtney Love and Richard Gere.[2]

> *Life* magazine featured prayer in its March 1994 issue. "The Power of Prayer: How Americans Talk to God," announced the cover, along with a heartwarming picture of a child praying. But the smorgasbord of comments on prayer covered the religious waterfront. Featured were devout Christian and football coach, Joe Gibbs, Geraldine Scott, a Nevada prostitute, and Unitarian author Robert Fulghum.

Fulghum observed, "I don't pray to an entity. My thoughts are of being at home in the universe ... There is no 'other' to address," concludes this best-selling writer.[3]

Spirituality today can refer to a renewal of interest in ancient rituals, even ancient music. Topping pop music lists for some time was a Gregorian chant compact disc done by Spanish monks. Who would have believed that Gregorian chants would become top pop? My college-age son tells me it's good music for studying!

> Spirituality today involves a huge interest in near death experiences, wellness and naturopathic medicines, meditation techniques, yes, and angels. Not only have there been documentaries, movies on the subject of angels, but in many bookstores angels now have their own section. Almost seven in 10 Americans say they really believe in angels, and one third say they've felt an angelic presence in their lives. Angels, said a PBS documentary,

Spirituality in a Mixed-Up Age

are an important dimension of "the mystery of the spiritual."
Spirituality today is hot as well as hyped in the media and through Madison Avenue. It's a commodity that sells; however, the hyped spirituality of today is riddled with half-truths.

Popular Spirituality is Often only Half True

Take, for example, the highly publicized angel craze. Some today call angels "agents of divination," that is, agents who help one delve into the future through occult practices. Some urge us to call down angels to enter our bodies. The idea of a "guardian angel" has been transformed into something akin to the occult "familiar spirit."

Do I believe in angels? Of course! Do I buy into everything about angels sold by popular spirituality today? Absolutely not!

As we've already observed, the quest for spirituality today moves some Americans in the direction of Eastern religions, including pantheism, ideas of karma, reincarnation, and absorption into an impersonal God. Other people have sought spirituality by turning inward, either through drugs or some form of meditation. Some have invested themselves in the human potential movement, with its promise that we have within ourselves all the spiritual resources we need. Many people's quest for spirituality today sweeps them into the New Age movement. Michael Green says, "New Age is undeniably one of the most serious competitors which Christianity has had to face since the days of the Gnostics, who were in many respects its forbears."

The meaning of spirituality today can be very slippery. It can mean anything and everything, thus spirituality can really mean very little. TV journalist Bill Moyer claims that the struggle to define what it means to be spiritual is the biggest story of the century.

12

Hot, Hip and Half True

What is Authentic Christian Spirituality Today?

Authentic Christians today learn from the history of spirituality. Biblical Christians in the '90s need to learn from the mystics and contemplatives of yesterday.'''

We may learn from at least six traditions of Christian spirituality.[5]

1. In *Desert* spirituality, the emphasis was on the renunciation of the world in favor of silence and solitude of the desert. In a noisy and crowded society, silence and solitude are an essential part both of authentic Christian spirituality and one's general health.

2. The *Eastern Orthodox* tradition of spirituality stresses a mystical approach to God along with the unknowability of God. According to an eastern "saint," "One does not know God except in terms of our incapacity to apprehend him."[6] Healthy Christian spirituality contains a strong sense of mystery, wonder, and a realization of the limits to our knowledge.

3. *Monastic* spirituality attempts to foster the life of the spirit by providing a regular liturgical framework, along with other disciplines of communal life. Authentic Christian spirituality is never individualistic, but is always lived out within the Christian community.

4. *Fourteenth-century Mystical* spirituality involved a flowering of mysticism and spiritual guidance by writers such as Julian of Norwich and Thomas à Kempis, who are still known and read today. Christian spirituality is aided by wise guides. Many Christians today are returning to an appreciation of the "spiritual director" role.

5. There was also *Counter-Reformation* spirituality. In response to the Protestant Reformation, an intensity of spiritual fervor and activity arose within the Roman Catholic Church, il-

Spirituality in a Mixed-Up Age

lustrated in Ignatius Loyola, founder of the Jesuit movement and other spiritual activities. Spirituality and activity today need never be divorced.

6. Finally, we may learn from the *Holiness/Pentecostal* tradition of spirituality, which is "more recent in origin, though the experiences which gave it birth lie deep in Christian spiritual history."[7] Intense prayer and praise, along with an emphasis on the Person and Work of the Holy Spirit, are its assets. These are always important dimensions in the life of the spirit. Its potential liabilities include lack of balance and self deception.

An authentic Christian spirituality today must also be *biblically orthodox.*

Biblical Christians *do* believe in the world of the spiritual.

Biblical Christians *do* believe in an unseen world.

We *do* believe in spirituality.

But at the same time, we *don't buy* into anything and everything bearing the label "spiritual." We need to recognize the presence of half-truths in our culture's lurch toward "spirituality." While we take issue with half-truths, we do well not to throw out the proverbial baby with the bathwater. We bring everything, including contemporary ideas about spirituality, to the revelation of God in Scripture and in Jesus. This enables us to make sense of the current rage over spirituality.

"Discover what Scripture says about spirituality and immerse yourself in it," urges Eugene Peterson. "This is not," he adds, "a matter of hunting for a few texts, but of acquiring a biblical imagination → entering into the vast world of the Bible and getting a feel for the territory, an instinct for reality."[8]

Authentic Christian spirituality today is *Spirituality with a capital S.* Much of what people today call "spiritual" has

Hot, Hip and Half True

to do only with the human spirit. It is spirituality with a small s. It is spirituality "from below," that is, from a merely human perspective. It is the developing awareness of our interior selves, the inside of us, where, many say, we make contact with our higher power, "the force," or God, who often turns out to be little beyond an extension of human self.

Uniquely Christian spirituality, however, has to do with a capital S. It is God's Spirit at work in and through our human spirits. Biblical Christians do need to be more aware of the interior life, affirming and celebrating the potential of that life. But biblical Christians always speak of that interior life in relationship to God; God's Son, Jesus; and God's Holy Spirit.

Furthermore, authentic Christian spirituality in the '90s will *affirm the hunger for God and spiritual experience,* expressed in today's popular quest for spirituality. We know that "our hearts are restless until they rest in thee," as St. Augustine put it. We also know that human hunger for God can lead questing souls to the junk food of half-truths, with something less than authentic Christian spirituality.

Spirituality, as defined by Henri Nouwen, is "what we know by heart." Thus, in the following chapters, prepare to open up to deeper dimensions of life in relationship to Jesus Christ and life in process of transformation by the Holy Spirit. Prepare not merely to think about but to taste the realities of spiritual living, for spirituality is not merely something to be talked about but something to be tasted.

2

Something God Does

Gung ho Christian

Let me introduce you to a hypothetical, but real person I am calling "Gung ho Christian." This is a man or woman, who may have had a recent spiritual experience at a retreat or because of a turning point in life. Possibly, a tragedy has brought this Christian closer to God. This person is earnest about living out this newly made commitment.

Gung ho Christian asks, "What do I need to do to be a really spiritual person? What must I do to be a growing, maturing Christian?" How would we answer these questions? Wouldn't we tend to give Gung ho Christian a to-do list, usually ending with the word *more*?

Pray more.
Read the Bible more.
Be involved in the church more.
Witness more.
Serve the Lord more.

Maybe some of us see ourselves in Gung ho Christian. Maybe some of us have received this kind of answer to our earnest quest. Maybe some of us have given such answers.

The idea is that if we *do* these things, *we* will make Christian growth happen, and that we will make ourselves spiritual people. These may be good and important things for Gung ho Christian to do, but the essence of Christian spirituality does

Spirituality in a Mixed-Up Age

not lie in doing more of these good things. They don't make spirituality happen.

Multitudes of sincere and well-intentioned people are weary of being told again and again what they must *do* to be good Christians. Some of them try to stick with the program and keep doing all the good things. But for some, the motivation wears thin.

Christian behaviors can become a thin veneer over a static, unsatisfying Christian experience. For many, there's the anxiety of "Am I doing enough? Is God pleased with my performance? What more should I be doing?"

Some stick with the program but do all the right things for inadequate reasons. They are like well-intentioned people who buy a bright, good-looking new car, but one which has no engine. They find they have to push and strain to get it to go anywhere, especially uphill.

Other Christians respond to a heavy diet of what they must *do* by tossing away the whole business of being a growing and spiritual person. They are weary of the pressure and tired of the constant weight of obligation. Some have become skeptical about evangelical Christianity and have turned for refuge to the New Age movement, to self-help therapies, to vague, permissive forms of Christianity without content, or to a completely secular spirituality.

Doing good things doesn't make spirituality happen. Authentic Christian spirituality is not primarily something we do, think or feel. It is not a technique, a philosophy or a set of disciplines. Christian spirituality is first and foremost something God does.

Geyser and Growth

It was a warm summer afternoon when my wife and I

Something God Does

turned off the main road in Yellowstone National Park to a side route leading to one of the geothermal areas. This was one of the fascinating, hot spots in the park. At one point, we saw a collection of stopped cars, a signal in Yellowstone that there's something neat to see → a herd of elk, a bison or a geyser about to erupt. This was the Great Fountain Geyser, which erupts only once in about 12 hours. A sign in the parking area noted that the geyser was predicted to erupt somewhere between 4:20 and 8:20 p.m. Since it was 5 p.m., we thought — *Well, maybe!*

The geyser pool, already filled to overflowing, was a good sign. Now and then, there was a little bubbling up from the left side of the pool which spread all the way across. When the boiling up seemed to begin in earnest, spectators came alive. But then, everything would settle back down again.

I thought to myself, *Why doesn't this thing get on with it? After all, I don't have all day to sit here and watch!* But then, the cycle of bubbling up at the left side and spreading across the pool would begin again, and I thought, *Maybe, now it will blow!* Mary Ann and I sat around and watched the pool hiss, steam, bubble and then subside for more than an hour.

I'm not good at sitting around and waiting for things to happen! Some people got up and left. We almost did. But experienced geyser watchers assured us the wait would be worth it. I heard one father trying to explain to his son, "This isn't a video game where you put in a quarter and something exciting happens. This is a geyser!"

It became apparent that there was nothing we could do to make the Great Fountain Geyser erupt, absolutely nothing! We couldn't hurry the processes of nature. *We couldn't make it happen!* Geysers are controlled by a force beyond us. Even the National Park Service sign says, "We predict. We do not schedule."

Finally ... finally ... the boiling up of the geyser pool be-

Spirituality in a Mixed-Up Age

came climactic and with a wonderful whooshing sound the eruption started in earnest. Much to the delight of those who had waited, a huge column of steam and water shot up at least 150 feet into the air. This particular geyser erupts in spasms. It spurts up a great column of hot water, subsides, and then does it again several more times. It was a magnificent eruption, and we had nothing to do with making it happen.

Growth in Christian spirituality is something (not altogether) like a geyser. It is organic not mechanical. It often takes time and is not under our control. There is no to-do list guaranteed to make it happen. And that's frustrating to Americans who are used to making things happen by our own efforts and on our own timetable. Oh yes, we can put on a veneer of spirituality by ourselves. If conformity to external standards and other people's expectations is what we mean by spirituality, then we can do that ourselves. But deep-down, Christian spirituality is not something *we* produce.

Can a Mother Make a Child Grow?

Change the picture from geyser to a growing baby, beautifully developing in a mother's womb. Can a mother do anything to enhance her baby's development? Of course! Nutrition, exercise, healthy lifestyle, medical attention — all respond to and assist that developing life in the womb. That child, however, is a gift from God.

I have noticed that pregnant women, especially those expecting their first child, often tell me with great confidence when their child will be born — the "due date." But you know as well as I do that this "due date" is an educated guess. Unless there is medical intervention, labor, delivery and birth are not absolutely predictable.

Once a baby comes into the world, the child grows ac-

Something God Does

cording to patterns built into the genes. Can the mother and father assist and encourage growth? Of course! But they cannot produce it.

Our younger child grew very slowly. We had him tested for abnormalities, fed him vitamins, and in general, did all we could to foster his growth. But, for his first years of life he was one of the smallest children of his age. There was nothing we could do to alter his biological timetable.

Physically speaking, although we respond to a child by assisting and encouraging growth, we do not make it happen. The same is true of spirituality. While we affirm and encourage the development of spiritual life, spirituality is something God does.

Ephesians and Spirituality

The epistle to the Ephesians is a powerful manual of Christian spirituality. The opening half of this great letter makes it clear that we can't be truly spiritual on our own. In fact, according to the apostle, we can have no spiritual life in ourselves. Apart from God, he says, we are dead, lifeless (Ephesians 2:1-3). But, writes Paul, God has showered us with the blessings of salvation in Jesus (Ephesians 1:3-14). These blessings are gifts, not something we can buy, earn or deserve. These blessings are the gifts of grace (Ephesians 2:8-9).

The Ephesian model of spirituality does not start with what we must do, but with what God has done for us and continues to do within us. We will look in greater detail at the explosions of blessing Paul describes and at God's grace to us in Christ in a subsequent chapter.

However, we do have a role in spirituality. Ephesians gets to our role mostly in the last half of the book. But that role is primarily to be receptive and responsive to what God has

Spirituality in a Mixed-Up Age

done and is doing. "Cultivate receptivity" is an important idea to Christians desiring to grow in spirituality.

The hinge verse of Ephesians is Chapter 4, verse 1, in which God's work in us, and our response to that work are brought together. "I urge you," Paul writes, "to live a life worthy of the calling you have received." Chapters 1-3 of Ephesians are about "the calling we have received." This is God at work in us. Chapters 4-6 are about the life lived worthily in response to that calling.

Four words summarize our response to the initiative of God toward us described in Ephesians.

The first word is *turn*.

– *Turn toward God in praise and prayer*. That's what the opening segments of Ephesians tell us we can do to be receptive to what God has done for us. "Praise be to the God and Father of our Lord Jesus Christ, who has blessed us ... with every spiritual blessing in Christ" (Ephesians 1:3). The Ephesian letter contains two prayers by Paul (Ephesians 1:17-23 and 3:14-21), along with a request for prayers on his behalf (Ephesians 6:19-20).

How do we participate in the process of spirituality? Orient ourselves toward God in praise and in prayer. A nonpraising, nonpraying Christian is like a child who refuses to eat, or like an adult who will not eat right. Such a person is impairing the natural processes of growth at work within.

Another word is *relationships*. *Invest in relationships* is the admonition of the apostle in Ephesians (Ephesians 4:2-3; 15-16; 25-32; 5:21-6:9). Authentic Christian spirituality is never individualistic. Instead, it is in the context of our relationships, especially relationships within the Christian community where God is at work in us, and where we respond to God's work in us.

22

Something God Does

A third word is *behavior*. *Behave in accord with who you are.* Let your behavior be in synch with what God is doing with you and in you. "You must no longer live as the Gentiles do," urges Paul (Ephesians 4:17). "Everything connected with your old life has to go ... Get rid of it. And then take on an entirely new way of life ..." (Ephesians 4:22-23, *The Message*). We do not make ourselves spiritual people by our behavior. But if spirituality is the work of God in us, then that work is assisted or impaired depending on the nitty gritty behaviors of our lives.

A new sign on the freeway recently caught my eye. Because of accidents involving road workers struck by motorists, speeding fines are now automatically doubled in areas where road work is taking place. I envision another big sign on the freeway of our lives: "Behave with care. God at work!"

One more word completes this brief summary of Ephesians' description of how we may participate with God in Christian spirituality. It is *fight*. *Give attention to the fight*, is what I hear Paul urging (Ephesians 6:10-20). Because Christian spirituality takes place in a world filled with evil, it involves a struggle, a fight.

Yes to God.
According to theologian Karl Barth the essential definition of Christian spirituality is "Yes to God." St. Francis de Sales' favorite prayer, in which he summed up the essence of Christian spirituality, was this, "Yes, Father, yes! and always yes!"

When you and I get up in the morning, before thinking about what we must do to be good and pleasing to God, we need to celebrate what God has already done. That's where Christian spirituality begins.

Garrison Keillor, tongue in cheek, announced to Seattle

Spirituality in a Mixed-Up Age

audiences recently that sinners made good citizens. It takes a big load of guilt to make folks sit on all those committees, Keillor suggested.

Celebrating what God has done for us in Jesus and through the Holy Spirit liberates us from lifelong guilt and shame. If we do sit on committees, it is for good and healthy reasons. When we pray and read Scripture, when we participate in the community of believers and involve ourselves in spiritual disciplines, when we obediently serve God with our lives, it is for good and healthy reasons.

An authentic spirituality can take a load off our shoulders and give us relief from the "tyranny of the should." Genuine spirituality can give a deep-down motivation to love and respond to God from the depths of who we are. It is saying a great, big "YES" to God.

Spirituality and Real People

3

Abraham: Yes to God's Call

C. S. Lewis is reported to have said, "The great sinners are made of the very same material as the great saints." The opposite is also true: The great saints are made of the same material as the great sinners.

Sometimes, we may get the idea that spirituality is only for the weird. We think it's for those who wander around in left field somewhere, for New Agers or devotees of eastern religions, or for unusually pious Christians who wear halos most of the time and always go to midweek prayer meeting.

But authentic Christian spirituality is for anybody. It is for *real people*. In fact, some of the most real people I know are folks in the Bible. Their imperfections stand out like sore thumbs. Their sins are not glossed over in the sacred story, but their lives were nevertheless used by God to accomplish His purposes. They were spiritual people. They loved God. They were friends of God.

I heard Eugene Peterson lecturing to pastors at Regent College in Vancouver, Canada, on the biblical story of David. He stressed the earthiness of spirituality. According to Peterson, one of our basic sins is to want to be spiritual, meaning not having to deal with our spouse, wipe kids' noses, or wash dishes. We want to get away from the earth. But, claims Peterson, the more Christian we become the more earthy we become. The characters of Scripture are earthy, that is, concrete, real. Their

27

Spirituality in a Mixed-Up Age

stories were lived out in a real-life context like our lives.

Let's take a quick trip through early Bible biography, pointing out some of the blemishes and blessings of four illustrative Genesis saints. Each of them was very human, very ordinary, very earthy. But each of them demonstrates at least one aspect of Christian spirituality.

Abraham and Saying "Yes" to God's Call

He wasn't a resident of a monastery somewhere. He was not on the periphery of life's action. In fact, he came from one of the great urban centers of the ancient world, a place called Ur of the Chaldees. He was an important businessman in his day, a substantial man, responsible for leading and managing people. He had his own private army, 318 armed, trained soldiers in his retinue. He was also a wealthy man, as they counted wealth in those days → in sheep and goats, in herds of cattle, in people responsible to him. But Abraham was also a man whose heart turned toward God, whose life said "yes" to God's call.

Abraham didn't live in a God-fearing family or community. Ur was the center of moon god worship. His father was a worshiper of idols, maybe even an idolmaker. Surely, Abraham himself started out as an idol worshiper. He lived before the days of any written Scripture, before today's fresh paraphrases of the New Testament, and before devotional books of any kind. There were no synagogues or churches, no Christian colleges, parachurch agencies, Christian counseling services, Christian publishing companies and bookstores, or Christian radio and TV. But when God called Abraham, Abraham listened and obeyed. Amazing!

I observe at least two things about this very real, down-to-earth, yet spiritual man. One is this: *The pattern of his life was saying "yes" to God.*

Abraham: Yes to God's Call

Abraham said "yes" to God's call despite the lure of security. Like most of us, I see Abraham as a man who would have found it easy to draw security from life's tangibles.

Possession, position, the people around us — these are tangible, known security factors. Abraham was called to leave all that and set out for an unknown future. He was to exchange what this world calls security for a different kind of security — covenant relationship with this God Who had called him and had promised him a future.

Now, Abraham didn't always trust fully in God for his security. There *were* times when fear got the better of him. But the pattern of his life was to say "yes" to God's call despite the lure of security and the pressure of ambition.

As his story unfolds, there was a turf dispute between his shepherds and those of his nephew, Lot. You couldn't succeed in that economy without adequate pasture. And who didn't want to succeed?

But when it came to a decision that the two livestock owners would have to split up and go separate ways, Abraham, the patriarch, deferred graciously to his younger relative. It was more important to Abraham to follow God's call than to acquire the best pasture land.

When Lot's newfound territory around Sodom didn't work out so well and he found himself a prisoner of war, Uncle Abraham had to come to the rescue with his private army. He attacked the rascals, liberated his nephew and all the other captives from Sodom. Then, the king of Sodom, freed by Abraham, offered him the spoil of battle. That's the way things were done in those days. Surely, that would have appealed to Abraham's businessman's ambition. But Abraham said a firm "no." In fact, he tithed the spoil first before turning it over to the king of Sodom, giving one-tenth of it to Melchizedek, king of Salem,

Spirituality in a Mixed-Up Age

and priest of the Most High God (Genesis 14:18-24).
 Abraham also said "yes" to God's call despite the cost.
 When God tested his servant by asking for his only son, his long awaited heir, this son through whom God's promise would be fulfilled, Abraham said "yes" despite the cost (Genesis 22). Clearly, God didn't want the sacrifice of Isaac. God just wanted to know that Abraham would obey regardless of what it might cost.
 Abraham's spirituality was expressed in his life pattern of saying a vigorous "yes" to God.
 While Christian spirituality is the work of God's Spirit in us, not something we do ourselves, we can nevertheless assist or impair, encourage or hinder what God wants to do in us. We do that by saying "yes" or "no" to God's call in our lives.
 During recent bad-news days in Haiti, I heard this piece of good news on a radio broadcast. It was the story of a Haitian boy, born and raised in the small town of Pinyon. The son of a pastor, Guy stood by his father's side one day as a sick person died. Guy promised God he would become a doctor and help his people. He took medical training in Haiti, interned in the United States, served as a doctor in the U.S. Air Force, and then began to enjoy the good life in America. But in 1983, he remembered his promise and returned to Haiti. Today, through his 30 bed hospital in up-country Haiti, Guy is saying "yes" to God's call. He's a real person today in the midst of a real and difficult situation, whose pattern of life is saying "yes" to God.
 Another dimension to Abraham's story emerges: *The promises of God were realized despite his failures*. In Abraham's life, there were some glaring failures to say "yes" to God.
 Instead of trusting God to do what He had promised, that is, provide a son and heir through his wife, Sarah, Abraham, following the custom of the time, took Sarah's maid,

Abraham: Yes to God's Call

Hagar, as his concubine. Ishmael was the outcome. The Arab peoples are Ishmael's descendants, and the offspring of Ishmael and of Isaac have been at each others' throats through much of history. Instead of waiting for God's timing, Abraham took matters into his own hands, creating a very difficult situation.

Twice, to save his own skin, Abraham jeopardized his wife, Sarah. Because his wife was a beautiful woman, Abraham was afraid some powerful ruler would kill him so he could add Sarah to his harem.

"I know what a beautiful woman you are," said Abraham to Sarah. "When the Egyptians see you, they will say, 'This is his wife.' Then, they will kill me but will let you live. Say you are my sister, so that I will be treated well for your sake and my life will be spared because of you" (Genesis 12:12-13). Don't you wonder what Sarah said in return?

Sure enough, Sarah did catch the attention of the Egyptian Pharaoh and this "sister" of Abraham was picked up, taken to the palace, and the "brother" was paid well for his "sister." While Abraham was contemplating his expanded bank account, God was inflicting Pharaoh's household with certain unspecified diseases. The ruler put two and two together and landed on Sarah as the cause.

"Why didn't you tell me she was your wife?" (Genesis 12:18-20). And the pagan king gave righteous Abraham a lecture on ethics.

The odd thing is that it happened again this time with a Philistine king named Abimilech. Again, a pagan king had to lecture righteous Abraham on his behavior (Genesis 20:9-10).

Abraham sounds like me! He has a hard time learning from a mistake. Can you identify with this ordinary person? But, despite these failures and a few others implicit in the story,

Spirituality in a Mixed-Up Age

God's purposes worked out, and God's promises to Abraham were fulfilled.

God apparently doesn't require perfect people to get His work done. And am I ever glad! God requires people whose pattern of life is to say "yes" to Him. I can hinder the work of God if my failures are willful and persistent. But if the pattern of my life is to say "yes" to God's call, His purposes and promises can be fulfilled even though I fail.

Abraham and Sarah and Waiting on God

Authentic Christian spirituality involves a pattern of saying "yes" to God's call, a pattern through which God works despite our failures and weaknesses. It also usually includes periods of waiting for God.

Americans are not good at waiting. We want things to happen now if not sooner. We're into the instant, the speedy, the express, the fast. McDonalds and drive-up service have become symbolic of our hurry-up approach to life. But being in a hurry is often not an asset to spirituality. God is not on our timetable. Have you discovered that?

Sometimes we pray and watch for an answer to our prayer. But the answer seems so slow in coming. When an answer does come, it may not be quite what we asked for. We are concerned for loved ones, watching for signs of spiritual development in their lives, yet we may see precious little spiritual progress. There are periods when God seems silent, even far away. We become weary of waiting for God. Yet, out of waiting for God there can come to us hurry-up people a deepening spirituality, which includes humility, patience and trust.

Here, again, is this man whom God called to leave his country, his people, his father's household and go to the land God would show him. God promised Abraham: "I will make you

Abraham: Yes to God's Call

into a great nation and I will bless you ... And all peoples on earth will be blessed through you" (Genesis 12:2-3).

When God called, Abraham said "yes." When God promised, Abraham believed. But time passed. The years wore on. One of the basic requirements for fulfilling God's promise is missing → a son, an heir, one through whom the calling and the promise could continue. Abraham, according to the custom of the time, offered to make one of his servants his heir. *Nothing doing, Abraham! A son coming from your own body will be your heir.* But though he and Sarah kept trying to have children, it wasn't working.

It was 10 years since Abraham and Sarah migrated to the land of Canaan, 10 years and more that they waited for children. They decided on a shortcut. Again, based on the customs of the time, Sarah pressured Abraham into using her maid, Hagar, as a surrogate mother. That doesn't work well today. It didn't work well back then, either.

I see pregnant Hagar beginning to put on airs around Sarah. "I can have babies and you can't! Ha! Ha!"

Despite the fact that Hagar was Sarah's own idea, I hear her blaming Abraham for the problem. "You did this to me!" she screams at her husband. "I want her out of my sight!"

What the Bible calls Sarah's mistreatment of Hagar, we, today, would call abuse. And all the while, Abraham seems to look the other way. Who says these aren't real people?

Hagar runs away but encounters God out in the desert. She returns to her mistress, tries to behave better, and finally Ishmael is born. By now, Abraham and Sarah have about given up on having their own child. Abraham is 86, Sarah, 76.

When Abraham is 99, almost old enough to get his birthday publicized by Willard Scott on the "Today Show," God had another life-transforming talk with His servant.

33

Spirituality in a Mixed-Up Age

"You know what, Abraham, Sarah's going to have a baby." None of this adopted servant business. None of this surrogate mother arrangement. "I will surely give you a son by her, by Sarah" (Genesis 17:16).

Abraham and Sarah waited almost 25 years for Isaac. The time-tested spirituality of these two very real people included the experience of waiting and waiting and waiting for God.

Time-tested spirituality involves at least two dimensions, as true today as they were 3,000 years ago. For one thing, their time-tested spirituality was *promise-based*. The focus of Abraham and Sarah's lives was the promise of God, part of which was fulfilled in their lifetime, but part still to come after they died.

Promise-based spirituality listens to God. Spiritual people are quiet enough to hear God speaking amid the noise outside us and the noise inside us. Spiritual people follow the example of the young boy, Samuel, who said to God, "Speak, for your servant is listening" (1 Samuel 3:10).

Promise-based spirituality looks to the future. Authentic Christian spirituality is always hope-filled, saying a firm no to the gloomspeakers and naysayers of today, because of eyes fixed on the promise of God.

Many weekday mornings I am at Green Lake, 10 minutes from my house in Seattle, for a three mile walk. Almost every morning I see people wearing walkmans while walking, jogging, biking or skateboarding. And often they're smiling! Who smiles at 6 a.m.? Occasionally you'll hear them humming or singing along to the music from their little radios. Christian spirituality involves living now to the music of God's future, God's promises. Other people may not hear the music we listen to. They wonder, "What's going on with these people?" But we're tuned in to the music of hope.

34

Abraham: Yes to God's Call

Not only is time-tested spirituality promised-based, but it is *persevering*. Abraham and Sarah didn't just sit still and wait for God to do something. They lived their lives fully. They persevered in doing what God said to do. Abraham kept building altars to this God Who had called him. He kept on with his livestock business. And he and Sarah kept trying to have the baby God had promised.

After describing and illustrating faith in Hebrews 11, this early Christian author urges us to "run with perseverance the race marked out for us" (Hebrews 12:1).

Sometimes Christian spirituality involves just sticking with it, regardless. It is doing what's right regardless of what we feel like inside and regardless of pressures from the outside. Spiritual people persevere in the purpose God has given them.

Spiritual people also persevere with people. We do not give up on other people, even though what we see right now is discouraging. Spiritual people are willing to wait, sometimes a long time for people to respond to God. We also do not give up on ourselves despite our own slowness to learn and grow.

Jimmy and Sheila had been divorced for 10 years. They had not spoken since the divorce decree, but Sheila had since come to faith in Christ. One day, she found herself talking long distance with her former husband.

"I know this will be hard for you to believe, Jimmy, but I've become a Christian. I am not calling to try to get back together. It has been too long. But I was thinking the other day about how much I must have hurt you when I left you 10 years ago. Maybe I'm asking the impossible, but I want to know if you could find it in your heart to forgive me."

There was a long silence on the other end of the line, finally broken by a sob. On a Saturday afternoon, six months

Spirituality in a Mixed-Up Age

later, Jimmy and Sheila were remarried. During the ceremony, sometimes they cried. But sometimes they laughed.

Waiting for God can be like that. Sometimes you cry because it's hard waiting for God's promises and purposes to be fulfilled. But sometimes you laugh because God is the eternally surprising One. After all, who would have thought Sarah would become the mother of Isaac? And who would have thought Jimmy and Sheila would get together again? You laugh because you get glimpses that God is at work even while we wait.

4

Jacob: Wrestling with God

Here's **another ordinary** person named Jacob. He's a man having a midlife crisis. At least that's what we'd call it today.

Jacob had made it big in business. To pacify his alienated brother, Esau, he selected from among his herds this present: 220 goats, 220 sheep, 30 camels with their young, 40 cows, 10 bulls and 30 donkeys. Some present (Genesis 32:13-15)! Jacob was a very successful man!

But Jacob's past haunted him. There were wounds caused by other people → his mother, his father, his brother, his father-in-law. He was brought up in a dysfunctional family and he lived in one, too. Making it big materially didn't compensate for the ghosts of Jacob's past.

Jacob's future frightened him. Moving back across country to his homeland meant having to deal with his brother, who had been murderously angry with him 20 years before.

Jacob's past and future met one dark night by the side of the river Jabbok. Having sent his family over the river ahead of him, Jacob was alone that night. Jacob remembered how close God had been to him once as a young man, so close he'd named the spot Bethel, or House of God. He'd put up a memorial marker at that place. If only he could feel God that close now! But all he felt were the ghosts of his past and the shadows of his future.

Spirituality in a Mixed-Up Age

Suddenly, there was a hand on Jacob's shoulder. Standing next to him in the darkness was a man. But Jacob could tell this wasn't just a man. This was God in the form of a human being. The Bible story says this man "wrestled with him till daybreak" (Genesis 32:24). This one night of wrestling with God expressed a lifetime of struggling with the Lord and with himself.

Maybe you've been where Jacob was that night. Have there been nights when you felt like you were wrestling with God, with yourself, with life issues all night long? It may not have been a midlife crisis. But what kinds of crises have you known? Do you know what it is to have your past beat up on you? Do you know what it is to have your future frighten you? It has been suggested that Jacob's great encounter with God came when he knew himself to be exposed to a situation wholly beyond him. Maybe we've been in situations like that.

Sometimes we wrestle with God over issues of obedience.

Often we wrestle with God at key points of life transition. Wrestling with God may take place in the context of suffering or adversity.

Wrestling with God and with real-life issues is key to a deepening spirituality. God is there in the crises of our lives, where we can respond to Him and become deeper, more mature persons. Joe Gibbs, former Washington Redskins head coach, and man of faith, once said, "God loves us in good times and bad ... But He is even more real in our lives when we are having tough times."

There were at least three outcomes of Jacob's wrestling with God. For one thing, *Jacob limped* for a while because of an injury sustained while wrestling. Wrestling with God and with real-life issues exacts a price. Real struggle with hard issues drains us emotionally, sometimes physically. Even Jesus, Son of God, "limped" in His wilderness encounter with the devil. After

38

Jacob: Wrestling with God

His time of temptation He was in such need that angels attended to Him. Jesus "limped" in the Garden of Gethsemane, where He wrestled with the decision of whether or not to accept the cross, and where His sweat was like great drops of blood falling to the ground (Luke 22:44). On the cross, "limping" in His sense of aloneness, Jesus cried out, "My God, why have you forsaken me?"

When we wrestle with God and with life issues, we may "limp" for a while. And that's OK. There's a human brokenness which is healthy. It signifies the defeat of arrogance and self-centered independence. It means we recognize our weakness and dependence upon God.

Another outcome of Jacob's wrestling with God was that *his name was changed.* Jacob, the deceiver, became Israel, the one who wrestles with God.

In ancient society, one's name and identity were closely linked. Jacob had a new sense of identity after wrestling with God. No longer did his self image revolve around deceiving. No longer did his past and his character flaws dominate his life. Now, his self image centered around the reality of having struggled with God over the real issues of life.

In Jacob's name change there was grace, the gift of a new beginning. That made the wrestling and the limping worthwhile.

One more outcome of Jacob's wrestling was that *he received a blessing.* Once before, Jacob had been blessed by his father, Isaac. But then, the blessing had been contrived, manipulated, brought about by deceit. It resulted not in genuine blessing, but the curse of having to leave home, the curse of alienation from his brother. This time the blessing was not just from father Isaac, but from the Heavenly Father. Jacob asked for God's blessing and he received it.

Spirituality in a Mixed-Up Age

People in the Wesleyan tradition have often seen Jacob's wrestling with God as his decisive time of entry into "the deeper life," the experience of "the second blessing," the blessing of a pure and undivided heart toward God. It is not unusual to find such an encounter with God following a time of crisis, a time of facing self and God.

Some time ago, I had the privilege of listening to Terry Waite. Terry was emissary of the Archbishop of Canterbury, and, in process of trying to negotiate the release of hostages, was himself taken hostage. For five years, he was a hostage — almost four of these years in solitary confinement. He had to wrestle to maintain his sanity, to keep his mind going, to keep hope alive, to prevent bitterness from destroying him. Obviously, he and his family wouldn't want to go through that ordeal again. But, said Waite, this big, but gentle-spoken man, "We came through that hard time in better shape than we were before."

5

Moses: Face-to-Face with God

One dark night, a mother told her young son to get the broom kept just outside the back door.

"But it's dark out there, Mom!" the little boy complained.

"It's OK," replied Mom with true adult logic, "God is out there and He'll not let anything happen to you."

Slowly, the little fellow went to the door, opened it a crack, and called into the darkness: "God, if you're out there, please hand me the broom!"

That's the way many people feel about God's presence. "Lord, if ... if you're really there ..."

A recent book describing "Generation X" speaks of the difficulty many 20-something adults have with the concept of a personal relationship with God. The authors claim that "the notion of God the Father has little meaning to large number of people, who grew up without a father." It's hard for such young adults to experience face-to-face communion with God. A young adult once said to me, "I wish ... just once God would speak to me so I could unmistakably hear Him."

"No prophet has arisen in Israel like Moses, whom the Lord knew face-to-face" (Deuteronomy 34:10). There is no greater commendation of any biblical person than this. God knew Moses face-to-face. Presumably Moses knew God face-to-face.

But what was there about Moses, which made possible

Spirituality in a Mixed-Up Age

this face-to-face relationship with God? Did Moses look and act like Charlton Heston in "Ten Commandments," where he is depicted as a superhuman, larger than life, unreal person? This epic movie notwithstanding, I am convinced Moses was a real person like you and me.

He was mostly reared by a foster mother. He grew up in a royal palace, which historically hasn't proved to be an ideal place for raising healthy children. He murdered an Egyptian and ran from justice for decades. He worked as a shepherd for many, long years – not a glamourous profession. He stuttered and wanted to use his speech impediment as an excuse for not obeying God's calling.

As an eventual leader, he thought he could do it all himself until he listened to his wise father-in-law's advice and learned to delegate. He became so angry at the Hebrews that he disobeyed God's specific instructions and struck a rock for water, instead of speaking to it. Moses was a real person all right! But yet, he was a real person who experienced face-to-face closeness with God.

There is no more central issue in Christian spirituality than face-to-faceness with God. This is, in fact, what we humans were created to enjoy. In the Garden of Eden, Adam and Eve walked and talked face-to-face with God in the cool of the evening. Genesis Chapter 3, however, describes the impact of sin in the world and in human lives. Sin leads to separation, to a barrier between human beings and God. Face-to-faceness with God is an experience to be reestablished.

Christian spirituality is God at work in us to overcome the impact of sin so that we may know Him face-to-face and live in intimate, personal relationship with our Creator. This is what God desires for us. And this is possible for real and ordinary people, like you and me.

Moses: Face-to-Face with God

But back to Moses. Here is this former Egyptian prince, now a fugitive from justice. He's under the influence and protection of desert tribes people. Moses married into the tribe and is now taking care of his father-in-law's sheep. It's just another ho-hum, boring day in the desert, herding those dumb animals as he's been doing for years. But on this very ordinary day, something unusual breaks into Moses' life. It is often when we least expect it that God transforms the ordinary into the extraordinary.

Moses sees a bush burning, nothing unusual in itself — maybe a lightning strike. But this bush isn't burning up! When Moses takes a detour to check out this unusual sight, he hears a voice out of nowhere. It was a voice calling him by name, "Moses! Moses!"

The only reason we can have face-to-face interaction with God is because this God knows our names. We are not merely a cosmic number to Him. We are not merely one of five or so billion occupants of a comparatively minor planet in one of millions of galaxies of planets. We are persons ≻ persons with names! I must confess, I feel good when the automatic teller machine knows my name! How much more impressive is it when the God of the universe knows me by name!

"Moses, I am God. And because I am God, the place around you is holy. Take off your sandals, Moses. You're standing on holy ground."

Then God said something Moses wasn't really interested in hearing. That often happens, you know. We may say we want to relate intimately and personally to God. But when God comes close, we're not really sure we like what He says to us.

"Moses, I want you to go back to Egypt and liberate your people in bondage back there."

"Who me?" was Moses' response. "God, You've got to

43

Spirituality in a Mixed-Up Age

be kidding! I'm just a shepherd. Since when has that been a stepping stone for leadership? And besides, maybe You've noticed, God, I have this speech problem. I couldn't lead people. And, God, one more thing, I don't know Who You are. If people say, 'What's the name of this God you're talking about?' What shall I tell them?"

"I AM WHO I AM" that's my name. This was God's answer to Moses. God has a name too. He's not merely a cosmic force or our "higher power." God has a personal name. And it's this God with a name, Who reveals Himself to us.

"My name is Yahweh-I am; I AM WHO I AM." I am the eternal and living God (Exodus 3:14). That was the way Moses began having face-to-face communion with God. Such interaction became a way of life for Moses, so much so that it could be said of him, "No prophet has arisen like Moses, whom the Lord knew face-to-face" (Deuteronomy 34:10).

Notice two perspectives on Moses and face-to-face spirituality. For one thing, *face-to-face spirituality happens because God shows Himself.*

Face-to-faceness with God doesn't begin with us and our search for God, or in our efforts to find and know God. Knowing God face-to-face begins with God's revelation of Himself to us. Authentic Christian spirituality begins when God speaks and tells us His name, when God tells us Who He is and what He is really like, when God tells us what He wants us to be doing. Face-to-face spirituality happens because God shows Himself.

But, someone says, I've never had anything happen like Moses' burning bush experience. I haven't heard God speak with an audible voice. Have you?

No, I haven't either. But God reveals Himself to those who look and listen. God has shown Who He is in nature — so

Moses: Face-to-Face with God

much so that the Apostle Paul told the Romans that people are without excuse for not knowing the truth about God (Romans 1:20). God has also shown Who He is and what He is like in Scripture.

But supremely, God has shown Himself in Jesus. The God of the burning bush says His name is "I Am Who I Am." Jesus, God in human form, said: "I am the light of the world. I am the bread of life. I am the way, the truth, and the life. I am the Good Shepherd. I am the resurrection and the life."

If we will look and listen, we will observe that the world is full of God showing Himself to us. Whenever we gather for worship, this God, revealed in His Son, is present to show Himself to us, to tell us His Name once more, and to tell us what He wants us to do. When we arise in the morning, this God, revealed in Jesus, is present to speak to us and to show us Himself and tell us what He wants us to be and do.

Ordinary people, real people can have face-to-face relationships with the God of the Universe, because this God chooses to reveal Himself, because this God tells us His Name, and because this God calls us to join Him in His great mission of liberating other human beings from bondage.

Face-to-face spirituality not only happens when God shows Himself to us, but also when we respond to that self-revelation.

Notice how Moses responded. These are responses, which 3,400 years later, still open us up to more and more of God's self-revelation so we, in fact, can relate to God face-to-face.

> One response is *reverence*. God told Moses to take off his sandals out of respect for the holiness of God. I'm sure Moses did so, right away! In the Middle East and East, even today, shoes are removed as a mark of reverence for holiness and for God.

Spirituality in a Mixed-Up Age

Even though we know God personally, we never get chummy with the Holy One. We do not approach God casually, clap God on the back, and exclaim: "Hey, good buddy, how are ya?"

It may sound like a contradiction, but yet, if we are really to know God personally, we must recognize that God is beyond our complete knowing. Later, when God appeared again to Moses, he was able to see only the back of God. Part of God's reality was hidden from Moses' sight and knowledge.

One of the biblical concepts we Westerners have trouble grasping is transcendence. God is near us, close to us, within us. But God is also above and beyond us. We can never fully and completely know God. If God were totally comprehensible by created human beings, God would cease to be God.

Human spirituality which responds to God's self-revelation must include reverence. That reverence incorporates deep humility in that we recognize there are limits on how much we can know God. We take our shoes off before God. We bend our knees. We respond to God's self-revelation with reverence.

Another response of Moses to God's self-revelation was obedience. After fussing and fuming and making excuses about how he wasn't up to it, and after asking if God wouldn't please send his brother to do his work, Moses finally did obey what God told him to do. He went back to Egypt and began the process, which would liberate the Hebrews from bondage.

Face-to-faceness with God is based on day-to-day obeying God. Often, our face-to-faceness with God is hindered and limited because we are unwilling to submit to God and do what He says. Obedience leads to greater and greater intimacy with God. Christian spirituality is enhanced and encouraged by ongoing obedience to what we know God is saying to us.

Moses: Face-to-Face with God

In Moses, there was a final and most important response to God's self-revelation. There was, above all, *love*. As Moses got to know God more intimately, he understood this truth more clearly. Later in his life, we read his mature reflections on what it takes to have face-to-face knowledge of God. These mature reflections are recorded in the Old Testament book that the New Testament quotes most often, Deuteronomy. When Jesus was asked which was the greatest commandment in the Law, He quoted from Deuteronomy: "Love the Lord, your God with all your heart and with all your soul and with all your mind" (Matthew 22:37).

Above everything else God wants us to love Him. Why? Because the very heart of God is love. God is power but loving power. God is holy but with a holy love, which, regardless of who we are or what we've done, reaches out to us and invites us and has compassion on us. If we love God with all our being, we *will* reverence God and we *will* obey God. The most basic, human key to face-to-face spirituality is loving God.

But how can we love God? We love God only when we catch a glimpse of His great love for us. "We love because he first loved us" (1 John 4:19).

Sometimes it feels hard to love God because we have the idea that God's love for us is like human love. It has to be earned. God won't keep loving me if I fail to be worthy of that love. We have few models of unconditional love in human life.

Sometime back, the news was saturated with the story of a mother willing to sacrifice her little children, apparently to enhance her availability to a man she wanted. Americans were horrified at a mother who could murder her babies. God spoke through the prophet, Isaiah: "Can a mother forget her little child? Yet, even if that should be, I will not forget you ... See, I

Spirituality in a Mixed-Up Age

have tattooed your name upon my palm" (Isaiah 49:15-16, *The Living Bible*).

It is in response to such love that we love God. And it is in our loving response to such love that we are able to know God face-to-face.

I wish I could tell you I always love God perfectly, that I always reverence God as God deserves, that I obey God perfectly. I wish I could tell you I always know God face-to-face. But I'm thankful that, as I keep my eyes on this self-revealing God, I grow closer to Him, and I know Him more and more completely.

I'm no Moses! I'm just Mark! But God knows my name. And God tells me His name, too. As I watch for this God in my life, and as I listen for Him day by day I increasingly know Him face-to-face. My spiritual life grows, and I fulfill the very purpose for which I was created, that is, to have face-to-face fellowship with my Creator.

God of the burning bush, Who showed Yourself to Moses;
God of the created universe, Who demonstrated Yourself in what You made;
God of the written Word, spoken in ancient times by prophets and poets;
God of the manger, the cross, and the empty tomb, Who supremely revealed Yourself in Jesus;
We take off our shoes in Your presence.
We bow ourselves in reverence and obedience before the revelation of Your being and character.
Thank You for calling each of us by name.
Thank You for wanting us to know You by name.
Thank You for wanting us to love You.
Thank You that even when we don't know You and love

Moses: Face-to-Face with God

You as we might, You continue faithfully loving us.
Help us to see You more clearly,
To follow You more nearly,
To love You more dearly.
This we pray. Amen.

6

Joseph: Living Our Dreams

C**hristian spirituality involves** accepting dreams God implants in our hearts and then letting God empower us to live out those dreams.

Joseph was a visionary. He started seeing visions early, as early as his teen-age years.

Joseph grew up in a big family, but it wasn't a big, happy one. There were two wives and two concubines, a potent recipe for unhappiness. There was a favorite wife and a favorite son. There was what we today call "sibling rivalry." In fact, Joseph's brothers didn't like him at all. It didn't help when father Jacob gave Joseph, his favorite son, a special, multicolored coat, not so much made for working as for showing off. How his brothers disliked this symbol of Dad's special affection for Joseph!

About this time, Joseph dreamed he and his brothers were binding sheaves of grain. His sheaf arose and stood upright. All the brother's sheaves bowed down to his sheaf. And this spoiled kid wasn't smart enough to keep this dream to himself for the time being. He told everyone about it! No wonder his brothers were furious at him!

Even his parents were irked at this kid's dreams. "Listen," Joseph told them, "I had another dream and this time the sun and the moon and the 11 stars were bowing down to me." It didn't take a psychoanalyst to figure out what that meant.

Spirituality in a Mixed-Up Age

"What is this dream you had?" his father scolded him. "Will your mother and I and your brothers actually come and bow down to the ground before you?" (Genesis 37:9-10).

Sometimes, when we first dream our dreams we're not mature enough to handle them well, and we brag about them. That's part of being ordinary real people. Christian spirituality, however, involves *handling our dreams humbly*. It is not particularly spiritual to brag about our vision of holiness and piety, about what we're going to do and be for God, about being more spiritual than others.

You see, the real hero of the Joseph story is not Joseph. It is God, whose hand was on Joseph, shaping him, molding him through time and circumstance. The real hero of our spiritual dreams should not be us but God. In contrast to Joseph, authentic Christian spirituality involves handling our dreams humbly, not being puffed up and proud because of them.

The Joseph story also makes it abundantly clear that Christian spirituality includes *persevering in our dreams despite difficulty*. In Joseph's life, there was one problem after another. He was sold into Egyptian slavery by his jealous brothers. After winning the confidence of his master, an Egyptian official, and being given considerable responsibility in his household, the sensual, but neglected wife of Potiphar accused Joseph of attempted rape. Thrown into prison because he would not yield to a woman's advances, Joseph spent years behind bars.

Finally, in Joseph's story, we see that spirituality involves *dreams progressively fulfilled*. Released from prison to become prime minister of Egypt, and eventually doling out food for his famine-struck family, Joseph and his brothers acted out in real life the dreams he had as a teen-ager. It is in the eventual fulfillment of our dreams that there is fruitfulness and blessing for others. That's the way it was with Joseph.

Joseph: Living Our Dreams

I'd *like to tell* you that if you just stick with your dreams, you'll see all of them fulfilled in your lifetime. But the truth is, there are some dreams which may not be fulfilled. We stick with them, nevertheless, believing God has ways of bringing those dreams to pass with or without us.

Dying Joseph gave instructions regarding his remains. "Don't you dare leave my bones in Egypt," he instructed his family. Why? Because Egypt is not where I belong, and because God is going to take my people up from Egypt to the land promised to our forefathers. That was Joseph's vision, but one he never saw fulfilled. Nonetheless, Jospeh lived his dream regardless. Many years after his death, his people *did* return to the promised land, and they took Joseph's bones to bury in Canaan (Genesis 50:24-26; Joshua 24:32).

Many centuries after Joseph, another visionary dreamer wrote to Christians needing encouragment to live out their dreams. Paul wrote to the Philippians: "I've got my eye on the goal, where God is beckoning us onward to Jesus. I'm off and running, and I'm not turning back. So let's keep focused on that goal ..." (Philippians Chapter 3, *The Message*). Spirituality is living on the basis of God-given dreams, God-given visions of reality, whether or not we see the complete fulfillment of those dreams in our lifetime.

53

Spirituality and the Growing Christian

(Meditations on Ephesians) 5

7
Saying Yes to God

A **little boy** kept falling out of bed at night. "Why do you think this keeps on happening?" his Dad asked. After some thought, the young fellow responded, "I guess I've just been staying too close to where I got in."

Spirituality is stymied when we stay too close to where we entered the Christian life. Under these circumstances Christian growth doesn't take place. A contemporary Christian writer has pointed out that spirituality is not *one* aspect of the Christian life. Rather, it *is* the Christian life. And Christian growth is at the heart of an authentic Christian spirituality.

But how should we understand spiritual growth? How can we be growing Christians?

Unfortunately, much of our thinking about spirituality and Christian growth revolves around what we must do. Manuals on Christian growth often contain fervent exhortations to do more of this and more of that good thing.

- Pray more.
- Read the Bible more.
- Attend worship more.
- Be of service to others more.
- Give more money.

These are good suggestions, but the essence of Christian growth and spirituality does not lie in doing more of these good things.

Spirituality in a Mixed-Up Age

The model of spirituality and growth suggested in the Epistle to the Ephesians, as we observed in Chapter 2, starts not with what we must do, but with what God has done for us and what God does in us. Our role is primarily to be receptive and responsive to what God has done and is doing. As observed earlier, to cultivate receptivity is important counsel for Christians desiring to grow in spirituality.

There are two words in the first two chapters of Ephesians which speak of what God has done. They are words which invite a response of, "Yes, Father, yes! And always yes!"

One of these words is *Blessings*. It's the key word in Ephesians 1:3-14.

These verses illumine the sky like one charge of fireworks after another, each exploding into brilliant colors. "Verbal rockets," is what Eugene Peterson calls them (unpublished lecture at Regent College, July 1994). The passage is one monstrous, undiagrammable sentence in Greek. Paul is so excited about what God has done that his language isn't neat and tidy, but rather extravagant in its expression. These are the spiritual blessings we have received and continue to receive through Christ. Take time to respond with awe and gratitude to each of them.

"He chose us in Him ... to be holy" (Ephesians 1:4).

There is mystery here about God's choice I can't claim to fully understand. This much is clear. It's not just that we choose God, like selecting one brand of cereal over another at the supermarket. Rather, it's God Who chooses us. God lays claim to us, and we respond to that claim by shouting, "Yes!"

Furthermore, it is God's purpose that all who believe in Him should be holy people. God chose us, in Christ, to be holy holy not just because we're good, but holy because we belong to God. We are His! That's the essence of holiness. We are cho-

Saying Yes to God

sen for a purpose, God's purpose, and that purpose is that we should be a holy people, a people, who reflect in our character the reality of belonging to God.

The next explosion of excitement is in verse 5. *"He des-tined us to be His children through Christ."*

Our destiny is to be part of God's great family of brothers and sisters in Christ. Furthermore, through us, His children, says Paul, great praise comes to God. And because we are His children, we have redemption, the forgiveness of sins.

We are chosen for God's purpose.
We are chosen to be His children.
Our part is saying "yes" and living "yes!"

Another rocket lights up the sky in Ephesians 3:9, *"He made known to us the mystery of His will."*

Mystery, in Paul's thinking, is a secret previously hidden from view, but now made known. Mystery is an open secret. And what is this now revealed secret? It is that God's will is to bring all things under one head, that is, under Christ. Christ is to be central in everything. As Paul put it in his letter to the Colossians: "He is the head of the body, the church; he is the beginning and the first born from among the dead, so that in everything he might have the supremacy" (Colossians 1:18).

One more verbal explosion, this time in verses 11-14. *"In Christ, we have obtained an inheritance."*

Because of what God has done for us in Christ, we are heirs. And that inheritance is stamped with God's seal of ownership, says Paul. Life in the Holy Spirit, which is what Christian spirituality is all about, is like a down payment on the full inheritance to come. What the Holy Spirit is doing in us today, making us more like Jesus, is just a foretaste of the full likeness to Christ that will be, a faint foretaste of the full inheritance.

Spirituality in a Mixed-Up Age

What do you do with an inheritance? Turn it down? Not likely. You say, "yes" and you receive it with thanks.

What do we do with the work of the Holy Spirit in us in the here and now? We say, "Yes, yes, God, thanks for working in me!"

Of course, I can say, "No thanks. Or yes, this, but not that!" I can hinder the work of God's Spirit in me by not cooperating and not saying "yes." But that's like rejecting the life-giving, health-supplying flow of water in a desert; like rejecting the gift of a great and life-transforming love.

The second word, which stands out in the opening paragraphs of Ephesians is *Grace*. It is the chief operative theme in Chapter 1:1-10. How often have we read or heard quoted the powerful words: "By grace you have been saved, through faith — and this not from yourselves, it is the gift of God — not by works, so that no one can boast" (Ephesians 2:8-9).

But in order to appreciate the wonder of this grace you have to understand our human need. If you are to appreciate a rags-to-riches story, you've got to see what the rags were really like. In the opening verses of Ephesians 2, the apostle pulls no punches to describe how badly we need God's grace, expressed in Jesus.

Apart from God's grace, he says, we are spiritually *dead*. There is no life of the spirit.

Furthermore, Paul tells us, we are *dominated* by evil and the evil one.

We are also *degraded* in behavior which is the result of this evil influence. We live merely to fulfill what Paul calls the desires of the flesh and of the mind (Ephesians 2:3).

The final statement of our plight — we are *doomed*. We are "objects of wrath," as verse 3 puts it. There are serious consequences of saying "no" to God.

Saying Yes to God

This is the predicament of human beings without God. This is why we need the grace of God. And this is an assessment of the human condition seldom seen in popular thought today. The New Age movement, following its predominantly Hindu line of thought, has an inadequate view of sin.

One person has paraphrased Paul: "Immense in mercy and with an incredible love, he embraced us. He took our sin-dead lives and made us alive in Christ" (Ephesians, Chapter 2, *The Message*). That's the gift of grace. And what do you do with such a gift? It only makes sense to receive grace with gratitude. One theologian has put it this way: "Above all else, grace ... and gratitude – our response to the grace of God – are the two most essential components of an authentic Christian spirituality."[1]

The hymn writer wrote:
"O, to grace, how great a debtor,
Daily, I'm constrained to be ..."
Yes, grace does make me feel like a debtor.

Yes, grace does motivate me to do good things and to live in accord with the great gift I have received. The reason, then, that I do those good things and practice those Christian disciplines is out of grateful response to what God has already done for us. Otherwise, we risk an anxious, stress-filled do-goodism or even a skeptical rejection of the Christian life.

A young Japanese woman from a Buddhist background talked to me recently about her impression of Christianity, an impression she had gained primarily by talking to Christians, she said. Her impression was that Christianity was keeping a set of rules. Only then would God love and accept her. I was glad to affirm that God's love is unconditional and that what she had understood as rules are really guidelines for living for those who have received the wonder of God's grace. She is even now deciding whether to become a Christian.

61

Spirituality in a Mixed-Up Age

Do you struggle with obligations and oughts in the Christian life?

Do you find yourself sweating and fretting to do this and that for God?

Lay again the basic foundation of saying yes to the grace gift of God. Practice responsiveness to what God has done for us. Let that be the basic foundation of spirituality and the growing Christian life.

"Grace," writes Thomas Oden, "is the unheard note in the strident chorus of literature on spirituality and moral development." He continues: "Christian spirituality quietly thrives on grace. The empowerment of the languid human spirit comes by grace."[2]

8

Living in Community

A research team studying American lifestyles met a young nurse, named Sheila. "I believe in God," Sheila told her interviewer. "I'm not a religious fanatic," she continued. "I can't remember the last time I went to church. My faith has carried me a long way. It's Sheilaism. Just my own little voice."

Eighty percent of Americans agree that an individual should arrive at his or her own religious beliefs independent of any churches or synagogues. Much of the pseudo-Christian or secular spirituality, popular today, is highly individualistic in nature. Even American Christianity stresses the personal pronouns and involves a kind of me and God and nobody else connection.

We also live in a day when it's hard to be a community. Contemporary culture tends to polarize people. We run to opposite extremes and shoot and shout instead of conducting civil conversations about issues. Even among Christians there is pressure to get on the bandwagon, use the right slogans, defeat the enemy by whatever means necessary, even if that "enemy" is part of the Christian community.

Not only is it difficult to be a community these days, but there are no perfect Christian communities in sight. It's not hard to see what's wrong with the church, any church. But better the church we have than no church at all. Writes Chuck

Spirituality in a Mixed-Up Age

Colson: "... The church is like Noah's Ark: the stench inside would be unbearable if it weren't for the storm outside. This is the church we have. And as imperfect and even repugnant as we find it at times, we need to acknowledge that it is through this church of fact that truth is being proclaimed and portrayed."2

I used to think of Christian growth and maturity as a solitary achievement by individuals who prayed much, read their Bibles a lot, worked at the spiritual disciplines vigorously, and served the Lord fervently. My models were spiritual giants who, seemingly at least, walked with God in solitary spirituality. I admired such people who seemed to fight their way to spiritual maturity, defeating the world, the flesh and the devil all by themselves.

But I was wrong! That is not a biblical or a Christian model. The culture out of which the Bible came to us was profoundly communal in its orientation. People saw themselves not just as individuals, but as members of the wider community.

Spirituality, as Eugene Peterson describes it, is "the alert attention we give to a living God and the faithful response we make to him *in community*."3

"Scripture knows nothing of solitary religion," wrote Bruce Milne. "The salvation it witnesses to is emphatically one which has corporate dimensions."4 Nobody put it more pointedly than John Wesley in his oft quoted saying, "Holy solitaries is a phrase no more consistent with the Gospel than holy adulterers."

One of Wesley's major contributions to the church was an emphasis on small groups, on the nurturing environment of a cell group. At the core of the Wesleyan movement were what he called "class meetings," regularly meeting groups of about a dozen people who participated deeply in each other's lives and who experienced an intense sense of community.

Living in Community

It is in the believing community that prayer and worship are offered to God. Even when in solitude Christians pray in community. We are part of a community and pray as members of it, even when we pray alone. It is in this believing community that an authentic Christian spirituality is nourished. This, too, is the message of Ephesians.

Ephesians is a letter about the forming of God's new society in the midst of the old, God's new community right in the middle of the world's chaos. Ephesians is about growing Christians but not just individually growing Christians. It is, rather, about the community of growing Christians.

A bird's-eye view of Ephesians highlights at least four pictures of this community-based spirituality which fosters the growing Christian life.

First, in Chapter 2:19-22, the apostle talks about being *built together*. The picture is of *construction*.

The apostle describes a building, in which God lives by His Spirit, a building which becomes a holy temple, and a building in which Jesus is the Cornerstone, with the apostles and prophets being its foundation. In this building, both outsiders, the Gentiles, and insiders, the Jews, who historically experienced alienation and enmity are made one through Christ and together become part of this great building's superstructure.

Have you ever been introduced to the game of Jenga? You start with a small tower made of crisscrossed, wooden blocks. The idea of the game is for each player to detach one of the blocks and place it on top of the tower. But you do it carefully, so the whole tower doesn't fall down. The goal is to see how high you can get as you remove the blocks from the lower levels of the tower and build them into a higher and higher structure. As we played this game at a family Christmas gathering, I observed that there really are no winners or losers. The

65

Spirituality in a Mixed-Up Age

person, whose turn it was when the tower finally fell down, was a kind of loser. But we all helped each other. We gave advice on which block to try to remove. We encouraged each other and groaned together when the tower fell regardless of whose turn it was. It was a community project to build a tower without knocking it down.

Christians are being built together, not just as a game, and not just to form a higher and higher structure, but into a building for God's purposes and His glory. This construction project involves us all. We all hold our breath when one player has a difficult move. We all cheer each other as we work together. We all mourn when there's a fall. We are being built together.

Another picture of Christian community, this time in Ephesians 4:14-16, is of *bodily growth*. There, the apostle speaks of *being lovingly truthful*. "Speaking the truth in love, we will ... grow up ..."

In the physical arena such growth is dependent on the family and on the wider community. Have you noticed that babies don't take care of themselves? The development of an infant happens only when the community works together to meet its needs. So it is in the spiritual arena. Spiritual growth comes not in isolation or in a vacuum, but out of truthful, loving relationships. According to Paul as each part of the community does its part, the community grows.

Our community is to be characterized by truthfulness, not just speaking the truth, but acting truthfully. The apostle is speaking of honesty between fellow believers, of honesty with one's self, of integrity, of reality. The Christian community which fosters growth is a community governed by truth. It's not one in which people pretend things are better than they really are. It's not one in which everybody puts on a happy face and

66

Living in Community

gives testimonies about glorious victories in Jesus. It's a community honest about life's tough places, life's failures, and life's hurts.

But such truthfulness is to be lived in the context of love. "Living truthfully in love, we grow ..." Truth, you see, is not just being right and using one's rightness as a club to beat other people over the head. Truth is not just holding correct doctrine and making sure everyone who thinks differently knows he or she is wrong. Writes John Stott: "Truth becomes hard if it is not softened by love: love becomes soft if it is not strengthened by truth." It is that kind of loving truthfulness which is the soil out of which Christian growth takes place.

Another Ephesians picture of the Christian community has to do with clothing. The picture, in Ephesians 4:20, is of removing dirty clothes, inappropriate for who we are. In the metaphor of clothing, the apostle is talking about *barring anti-community characteristics*.

You have, says Ephesians, "put on the new self, created to be like God in true righteousness and holiness." Therefore, because of who you are, "each of you must put off," like a dirty, inappropriate garment certain attitudes and actions, which work against community.

In the verses following Ephesians 4:25, the writer identifies some characteristics, which are to be barred from the life of the community if Christian growth is to be fostered.

- There is false speaking, an offense against other members of the body.
- There is unmanaged anger, which can lead into sin.
- There is unwholesome talk, which doesn't build up and which grieves the Holy Spirit.
- There is an unwillingness to forgive one another that ignores how we have been forgiven by God.

67

Spirituality in a Mixed-Up Age

- There is sexual immorality that is not just a personal wrong but a community offense. These days, we are told that certain "victimless crimes" are nobody's business but the couple's. Not so in the Christian community!
- There is obscenity, coarse joking, which, says Ephesians, is out of place among God's people.

Read these pointed verses that describe the kinds of attitudes and actions, that work against community. We need to bar from our lives and our community these anti-community characteristics, stripping them off like dirty, inappropriate clothes.

The final picture of community in Ephesians is of prayer. The apostle writes Ephesians from prison. "Pray for me," he urges in Chapter 6:18-20. When I think of intercessory prayer, the image which comes to mind is that of lifting up or bearing up another person before God. That is what members of the Christian community are to do for one another. And, in that bearing up of one another in prayer, we all grow.

The people of Israel, on their way from Egypt to the Promised Land, are engaged in a crucial battle. From a hilltop overlooking the battle, Moses stretched out his hands, presumably in prayer. According to the story in Exodus 17, as long as Moses holds up his hands the battle goes the Israelites' way. But when Moses lowers his hands in fatigue, the Amalekites start to win. Moses is accompanied by two colleagues, Aaron and Hur, who find a rock for the leader to sit on, and then hold his hands up, one on either side of him until the battle is finally won by Israel.

Community life involves recognition that we do need each other. We desperately need the supportive bearing up of the community in prayer.

Living in Community

So what's the bottom line on spiritual growth and the community? I offer four exhortations:

1. We need to avoid being lone-wolf Christians. To be a Christian is to be in community. We need to recognize and live that way.

2. When the community gathers for worship, we need to be there. This is not consumer-based entertainment — the "Sunday Morning Variety Hour." This is the gathering of the community to honor its Divine Head.

3. We need to be part of a smaller group of Christians who know us, care about us, and to whom we have some accountability.

4. Finally, we need to do all within our power to foster an atmosphere of love in the church. It is that atmosphere, which fosters spiritual growth.

9

Indwelt by God

Several years ago, a young American named Bruce Olsen risked his life to reach a primitive tribe of people in South America with the gospel of Jesus. After living among them, he found he had an unexpected problem — these people were too good. They didn't steal from each other. Marital infidelity was unknown among them. They didn't squabble among themselves, and they didn't drink or smoke. How could he preach sin and salvation to such a good people?

One day, however, the young missionary came across an Indian crying and calling out into a large rectangular hole in the ground. The man, he found out, was calling on God. These people, Olsen discovered, believed they had once known God. But a deceiver had come promising to lead them to a better hunting ground, and had instead led them away from God.

Here, then, would be the young missionary's approach with the gospel. Moral as they were, these people did not know God. Realizing that, they were unhappy. Because they were created in the image of God, they needed to know Him personally to experience life at a more fulfilled level. They needed to have God Himself live in them. This approach was so successful that close to 9 of 10 of these tribespeople trusted in Christ.

Great Christian thinker Blaise Pascal once said, "There

Spirituality in a Mixed-Up Age

is a God-shaped vacuum in every human heart." St. Augustine wrote of the human hunger for God, "Our hearts are restless until they rest in thee." The editor of a business magazine asked this question, "What good is lolling in your jaccuzi in the beautiful backyard of your breathtaking home if you feel an aching emptiness in your innards – a chronic pain that all the wine coolers in the world can't numb?"[1]

One reason spirituality is hot and hip these days is the hunger of men and women for God. Unfortunately, much of contemporary spirituality focuses only on the human spirit. It is spirituality with a small s. Authentic Christian spirituality, however, has to do with the Spirit – capital S – the Holy Spirit, Who desires to satisfy this inner craving for God. To do this, God offers not just ideas about God or a religion based around God, but God Himself. God offers to be personally present within each one of us.

To be a growing Christian is to hunger and thirst for the indwelling of God and to live on the basis of this indwelling day by day.

Paul's prayer in Ephesians is that, "Christ may dwell in your hearts by faith" (Ephesians 3:17). The two prayers of Paul in the opening half of Ephesians are prayers for the indwelling of God. He prays that you "may be filled to the measure of all the fullness of God" (Ephesians 3:19).

Everybody's filled with something, the apostle observes. With some people it is wine. Among you, he urged, be filled and keep on being filled with God's Spirit (Ephesians 5:18). In the prayers of Paul in Ephesians 1 and 3, there are at least two words summarizing his prayer for them – the *divine indwelling*. A third word gives insight into how we may, in fact, experience the indwelling of God.

72

Indwelt by God

Knowledge

Paul's prayer is that these Christians, "may know him better" (Ephesians 1:17). The indwelling of God and knowing God go hand in hand. This, of course, is not just knowing about God. It is not just knowing and accepting what evangelical Christians believe. This is knowing God personally. "A little knowledge of God," wrote J.I. Packer in his excellent book, *Knowing God*, "is worth more than a great deal of knowlege about Him."

In Paul's thinking, there are at least two qualities that accompany knowing God personally. One is *hope*. His prayer is that the Christians in Ephesus "may know the hope to which he has called you ..." (Ephesians 1:18). To know God personally is to look to the future with eyes bright with expectation and hope.

But someone objects, "You don't know my situation. You don't know how difficult my life is. You don't know how hard it is for me to respond to my life-situation with hope." One writer has responded to such a perspective this way, "It is not the way we deal with our human situation that is the basis for hope → hope is the basis for how we deal with our human situation. In other words, our circumstances are not to be our basis for hope. What is happening around us may not lead us to be hopeful. Rather, it is knowing God that is the basis for a hope-filled dealing with our circumstances.

Love

To know God is also to experience love. In Ephesians 3, Paul prays that through knowing God better, his readers might "grasp how wide and long and high and deep is the love of Christ, and to know this love that surpasses knowledge" (Ephesians 3:18). To know God is to know that we are loved,

73

Spirituality in a Mixed-Up Age

deeply and personally, unconditionally, faithfully by the God of the universe.

In ancient Palestine, one could buy two sparrows for one penny. If one was prepared to spend two pennies, the return was not just four sparrows, but five. The extra sparrow, thrown into the bargain, was quite worthless. But even that extra, "bargain" sparrow mattered to God. Even what was regarded as worthless counted with God, according to Jesus, "You are worth more than many sparrows" (Matthew 10:31).

To have God indwelling is to know God. To know God is to experience His love. To experience God's love is the basis for being a growing Christian.

Power

A second quality for which Paul prayed as he thought of the Ephesians being indwelt by God was power. He prayed for the empowering of their lives so that they might really live. His power, he says, "is like the working of his mighty strength, which he exerted in Christ when he raised him from the dead ..." (Ephesians 1:19-20). This is resurrection power, life-transforming power, and it is available to us because God indwells us through the Holy Spirit.

Listen again as Paul prays "that out of his glorious riches he may strengthen you with power through his Spirit in your inner being" (Ephesians 3:16). The Greek word for power Paul uses here is the basis of our English word "dynamite." Inner dynamite — that's what the indwelling of God is. That's what we need in order to deal with complex issues and difficult people. Isn't that what we need to be the kind of persons God intends us to be and the kind of persons we want to be? This is the power available to us because God indwells us through His Holy Spirit.

74

Indwelt by God

At my home in Seattle, I have two options for watering the flowers I have planted outside in pots and boxes. Sometimes I use a green watering can. When I fill it with water, it is full. But when I pour the water out on thirsty plants, it becomes empty. Most often, however, I water with a hose. When I connect the hose to the source of water supply, I find it is always filled with water ready to be used as needed. Authentic Christian spirituality involves connecting with this personal power and staying connected.

Prayer

"Hey, wait a minute," somebody says. "If God indwells my life, why do I struggle with being hopeful? Why do I have a hard time feeling loved by God? Why do I seem to have such little inner dynamite?"

How does this indwelling of God get translated into real life?

The key to experiencing the wonder of God indwelling us from day-to-day is what Paul is showing his Ephesian friends. He is in prayer. Prayer is the key to drawing on the resource of God within us. "Pray continually," Paul wrote to the Thessalonians (1 Thessalonians 5:17).

The kind of prayer I'm talking about is not making speeches to God from some kind of sacred, kneeling posture. It is, rather, a conscious awareness of God's presence and a life lived on the basis of that presence. Because I believe so strongly in the presence of God within me, I come back again and again during the day to brief prayers, which renew the connection between me and God within. And then, it's my challenge to live life on that basis. Getting up in the morning, going to bed at night, I acknowledge the presence of God. When my eyes are captured by beauty, when something wonderful happens, when

Spirituality in a Mixed-Up Age

love is given and received, I turn to God. "God, you are so good. Thank you for being with me and within me just now!"

Or "God, thank you that despite how I feel, this person is your creation and the object of your love. Because you live within me, you are going to help me treat this difficult person in a manner consistent with love."

When I do or say something not in accord with the indwelling presence of God, it is because I have not allowed that presence to be a magnet for my whole life by drawing me back in spirit to that inner reality of knowing God and being empowered by God.

David Hansen, pastor in a small town in Montana, has written helpfully on prayer in a book for pastors. What he says applies to all of us: "We need not whip ourselves with guilt because God wants us to pray all the time and we pray so little. Instead, we need to be acutely attentive to the presence of God. If we let go of our assumption that we know when to pray, and let God's presence draw prayer out of us, prayer becomes free, even friendly."[4]

Prayer at its most basic level is simply being in touch with the God who lives within. That kind of prayer, like an art or a skill, can be a growing reality in our lives. It is the heart of Christian spirituality and the key to being a growing Christian.

10
Integrating Faith in Life

One evening, I stopped at the church office. Since I had no appointments with people that evening, I was dressed in sweats and a baseball cap. I walked by the youth center door while our high school ministry team was in session. My unaccustomed pastoral look created such a stir that they sent the youth director out to get me to appear again in the doorway so they could see me in sweats and baseball cap. Some of the people in the church I serve, who see me only on Sunday, believe I wear a dark suit all the time! Sometimes, people expect the pastor to look like a pastor at all times!

The question I live with, however, is not so much what I wear when I'm in the public eye and when I'm not. The real question I live with is: Am I the same person in public as I am in private?

Billy Sunday used to say, "Reputation is what people say about you. Character is what God and your spouse know about you."

Do we find it difficult to avoid living a compartmentalized life? Do we have a face we wear at church, another for work, and still another for home? A comedian quipped, "Most Christians are people who spend six days sowing wild oats. On the seventh, they go to church and pray for a crop failure." Overstatement? Maybe, but we get the point.

An English aristocrat, after hearing a sermon by a fa-

77

Spirituality in a Mixed-Up Age

mous British preacher, commented, "Things have come to a pretty pass when religion is allowed to invade the sphere of private life."

Some people seem to think faith is primarily a ceremonial or ritual matter, not something which influences all we do. In these days of hue and cry over separation of church and state, we are sometimes told that one's faith is a purely private matter and has nothing to do with our politics.

The growing Christian life, portrayed in Paul's letter to the Ephesians, is spirituality integrated into the nitty-gritty of everyday life. The letter is addressed to "the saints" (Ephesians 1:1). But, instead of being pale-faced, halo-surrounded people from old-fashioned pictures, they were ordinary, everyday Christians, who faced the task of being spiritual in every area of life.

Ephesians is a letter calling for the integration of faith into one's whole life. The growing Christian life, as described here, is one in which God's grace and our response to that grace break down the compartments of our lives so that we are Christian through and through.

Listening to what Paul writes to the Ephesians, primarily in the last half of Chapter 5 and into Chapter 6, I observe two basic principles for the integration of spirituality into all of life.

The first principle is that *all of life is to be spiritual.* Not just spiritual in the vague, slippery sense in which the word is often used today. All of life is to be Spiritual → capital S. That is, all of life is to be under the influence of the Spirit of God.

A key verse is Ephesians 5:18 (*The Message*): "Don't drink too much wine. That cheapens your life. Drink the Spirit of God, huge draughts of him." When one is drunk with wine, the effect involves the whole person. Alcohol influences the brain and the brain our whole being.

78

Integrating Faith in Life

By contrast, Paul urges, let the Spirit of God Who lives within us have a positive and transforming impact in every area of our lives. Let the dominating principle of our whole lives be God's Holy Spirit. There is, then, no room for compartmentalizing life into sacred and secular, spiritual and unspiritual, work and church, home and school. Instead, our whole lives are the arena in which God the Holy Spirit is at work with our willing agreement and cooperation.

The concept of being filled with the Spirit is simple, though its implementation may take our whole lives to work out. Although the filling of the Holy Spirit takes place initially at a point in time, the bottom line of being filled with the Spirit is letting God and His Son, Jesus, dominate one's whole life. Let our relationship with God through His Son Jesus become so all-pervasive that God becomes the dominant force in us.

We will need and ask for special infillings of the Spirit for particular times and for special tasks. But the most basic understanding of being Spirit-filled is being full of God. The key to continuing to be full of God is a constant and open relationship with Jesus. This good-sense, life-affirming intimacy with Jesus is the heart of being filled with the Spirit.

In Ephesians, the exhortation to be filled with the Spirit is accompanied by specific descriptions of the outcomes in our lives of this experience. Living full of God extends into all of life:
- How we talk,
- Our emotional lives,
- Our sexual lives,
- How we relate to one another.

All of life is to be spiritual. All of life is to be under the dominating influence of God's Spirit through our relationship with Jesus Christ.

Spirituality in a Mixed-Up Age

A second Ephesians principle for the integration of spirituality into every area of life is this, *All of life is relational.*

Most of the real-life situations described in Ephesians into which spirituality must extend have to do with our relationships. Relationships are the basic stuff of life. They are central in spirituality, in Christian holiness, and central in Christian growth. But relationships are some of the most complex aspects of life. While they can be rich and rewarding, relationships can also be full of pitfalls, booby traps, mine fields.

I have found that even when I feel as full of God as possible, I can still blow it royally in a relationship. Some of the most godly people alive struggle with relationships. Some, who want to be considered spiritual, seem blind to the implications of spirituality in their relationships. How these ostensibly spiritual people treat other people leaves much to be desired. Since life is primarily relational, it is in my relationships that spirituality must work if it is going to work at all.

In Ephesians 5:22, Paul begins specifically to apply the exhortation to be "filled with the Spirit" to a series of relationships. Examples include: the relationship between husband and wife, parent and child, slaves and masters, or employers and employees. These listings, common to New Testament times, are sometimes called the household rules.

Sometimes, contemporary people get hung up on the authoritarian sounding tone of this passage. Wives, submit! Children, obey! Slaves, obey!

It all sounds so hard-nosed and not socially correct stuff for our day and age. I propose, however, that the real issue here is not the question of who is in charge. The real issue is how being full of God should influence the quality of our relationships. The exhortations, which control all that follows, are, "Be careful

Integrating Faith in Life

then how you live," (verse 15), and "be filled with the Spirit" (verse 18).

How should being filled up with God, which is the way Christians should live, impact the character of their relationships in marriage, the family, and the workplace? That is what the apostle is getting at here, not just the rather self-centered question of who is boss and who obeys whom.

How should our relationships reflect being full of God?
- One principle based answer is that: *We are all responsible to God for how we relate to one another.*

In the ancient world, when Ephesians was written, the person who had less authority in a relationship held the responsibilities. Wives had responsibilities to husbands, children to parents, and slaves to masters. But, Paul says that in Christ, everyone has relational responsibilities.

In addition to telling wives to submit to their husbands, which everyone in that culture assumed, Paul taught husbands that they had responsibilities, too. Husbands have the responsibility to love their wives as Christ loved the church. In addition to being a huge challenge for any generation of husbands, that was a revolutionary idea in an age in which the husband was absolute boss.

Fathers in the ancient world were responsible and had the last word when it came to their families, says Paul. They were and are responsible not to provoke their children to anger, and as the parallel Colossians passage puts it, responsible not to discourage them.

It's not just slaves who have responsibilities to masters. Masters also must not threaten, play favorites or forget they, too, have a Master in heaven.

Everyone in relationships has responsibilities to God for how they relate to one another.

Spirituality in a Mixed-Up Age

Another principle is that: *Mutual submission is the primary pattern for relationships.* "Submit to one another out of reverence for Christ," is the way Paul puts it (Ephesians 5:21).

Clearly, the submission doesn't just go one way. Husbands will also submit to wives, just as Christ submitted to the church by giving Himself up for her. Unfortunately, the relationships between men and women often degenerate into questions of power and control, into struggles about who is going to "wear the pants." That, however, is not the way Christian relationships are supposed to work. Submission to one another is the pattern.

Similarly, parents will also submit to children, caring for their children's needs. In Christ, masters will also submit to their slaves.

The issue is not primarily who is in charge but how to express our being full of God in relationships.

The final and most important principle: *Jesus is the model for how we treat one another.*

Jesus is the model for how full-of-God people act in relationships. Did Jesus have authority? Did Jesus exercise leadership? Could Jesus be tough, even stern when the occasion required it? But did Jesus not wash the feet of those whom He led? Was it not Jesus who said to His followers: "Kings like to throw their weight around and people in authority like to give themselves fancy titles. It's not going to be that way with you. Let the senior among you become like the junior; let the leader act the part of the servant ... I've taken my place among you as the one who serves" (Luke 22:25-28, *The Message*).

When we lead, it is to be by serving, by giving up our rights for the sake of the other. This is the way we integrate our faith into our relational lives. Jesus is the model for how we are to treat one another.

Integrating Faith in Life

Do we fall short of this ideal? I do. But just because the ideal is steep, and just because we don't always live it out, it doesn't mean we reject the ideal as the vision for our lives. It means that in our relationships, as perhaps in no other area of life, we need frequent forgiveness from God and from each other. It means that we acknowledge to God and to each other that we are travelers toward this goal, even though we haven't entirely reached it yet.

Max Dupree, Christian businessman, tells about his granddaughter, prematurely born, weighing only 1 pound, 7 ounces. She was so small that his wedding ring would slide up her arm to her shoulder. She was given only a 5-10 percent chance to survive the first three days. The birth father had walked out the month before, so the nurse told Max he would have to be the surrogate father for a few months. His assignment was to come to the hospital every day and rub her tiny body with his fingertips, while telling her how much he loved her. The words and the touch of love paid off. She lived!

Love is the key to human growth. Love is central in spiritual growth as well. Love is living out the indwelling fullness of God in every relationship.

11

Using God's Weapons

From three to five days of most weeks, I respond unwillingly, but obediently to the alarm clock at 5:40 a.m. With my running clothes on, and a quick cup of instant coffee, I drive eight minutes to Green Lake where I meet a friend for a brisk walk. One of the things I find myself saying as my complaining knees and sundry other joints begin to warm up is this, "Why is this still so hard?" After walking for more than 20 years, you'd think it would get easier. But no, it's still a struggle.

M. Scott Peck began his best-selling *The Road Less Traveled*, with this pointed sentence, "Life is difficult." He continued, "Most do not fully see this truth that life is difficult. Instead, they moan more or less incessantly, noisily or subtly about the enormity of their problems, their burdens, and their difficulties ... as if life SHOULD be easy." But, says Peck, "Life is a series of problems. Do we want to moan about them or solve them?"[1]

Maybe we do believe life is difficult. But do we also believe that the Christian life is difficult? Are we surprised when being a Christian is at least as hard, if not more difficult than the alternative?

Sometimes Christian people agonizingly say to me, "Pastor, why is it so hard?" They may be speaking of the reality that life itself is difficult. But sometimes, they're talking about spiri-

Spirituality in a Mixed-Up Age

tual struggles, about internal conflicts between doing what they know they should do and what their desires pull them to do.

Paul's final theme in Ephesians 6:10-20 relates to a basic characteristic of the Christian life, even of the growing Christian life, and that is *struggle*. In fact, Paul's metaphor is even stronger than that. He pictures the Christian life as a battle, as a war. The apostle began this letter with explosive ecstasies of wonder about "the blessings we have received in Christ." He closes the letter with a down-to-earth description of our struggle in living out those blessings day by day.

Some Christians contend that from the day they surrendered completely to Jesus the struggle ended. My response is, "Great!" But that's not most people's experience. Regardless of how complete our consecration is, most of us live with some level of struggle.

Christians have often understood the forces opposing the growing Christian life in terms of "an enemy troika," a threefold adversary.

The Christian's struggle is due to something within us that the New Testament calls *the flesh*. While the scriptural connotation of "flesh" is not always a bad thing, there are passages where "flesh" is used in a distinctly negative sense. *The New International Version* translation in these passages is "the sinful nature." In Galatians 5:16-17, for example, Paul sets up a contrast between two dominating life-principles. One is the Spirit, the indwelling Spirit of God Who moves us in God's direction, and Who, as we allow Him, progressively makes us more like Jesus. The other life principle is "the flesh." This is human life oriented around some center other than God, basically self-centeredness. The Spirit and "the flesh" lead in opposite directions. Thus, "the flesh" is an internal adversary. Putting this enemy to death is central to being

Using God's Weapons

a growing Christian. We must decisively reject "the flesh" and deal with it on the basis of its being dead (Galatians 5:24; Romans 8:13).

In addition to this internal adversary, there's an external enemy against which we struggle — *the world.*

"The world," as the New Testament sometimes speaks of it, is a good thing. God created and loves the world. A reading of the New Testament makes clear, however, that there is also a very negative use of "world." In this sense, it is human society alienated from God, human values in opposition to the values of God's kingdom, and human culture polluted by evil. James writes, "Friendship with the world is hatred toward God. Anyone who chooses to be a friend of the world becomes an enemy of God" (James 4:4).

Paul urged Christians in Rome not to be conformed to the world, (Romans 12:2) or as J.B. Phillips paraphrases him: "Don't let the world around you squeeze you into its own mold." The trouble is, we may not recognize how much we are being squeezed and molded by the world's values. We can be like the proverbial frog in a slowly heating kettle. We don't recognize our danger. We splash around pleasantly, not realizing we are threatened with being boiled alive.

It is "the world" that speaks to us through Hollywood's obsession with sex and violence, the media's particular twist to reality, and the advertising industry. Through creativeness this industry sends a message that emotional and spiritual needs can be solved by material means. That, of course, means we must buy, buy, buy! Remember the heartwarming Coca-Cola commercial about people from different races coming together, singing a wonderful song about perfect harmony? It makes you feel good all over until you recognize that the advertising message is that Coca-Cola makes peace happen. Hardly!

Spirituality in a Mixed-Up Age

It is "the world" that speaks to us out of the half-truths and distorted pictures of truth imbedded in popular American religion. Though 90 percent of Americans say they believe in God, the sense of personal sin has almost vanished from the positive, upbeat style of contemporary popular religion.

It is "the world" that speaks to us out of the distorted values so prevalent in our culture. It has been suggested that most middle-class Americans tend to worship their work, work at their play and play at their worship. As a result, meanings, values, relationships and lifestyles are distorted.

The more we are, in fact, growing Christians, the greater will be our sense of dissonance with the world. Thus, the greater the struggle is likely to be. It is all too easy to become so much a part of "the world" ourselves that the tension between the Christian life and "the world" is lessened.

A third element of the enemy troika, the one spoken of very clearly in Ephesians 6, is *the devil*. The apostle urges us to arm ourselves with divine resources so we can take our stand against "the devil's schemes" (Ephesians 6:10).

The devil literally means deceiver. Our deceiving adversary works through the internal impact of "the flesh," and through the external influence of "the world." The devil works through human self-centeredness, and through the false values of the world. That's why in Ephesians 6 the apostle implies that the devil is our ultimate adversary. "We are up against the unseen power that controls this dark world, and spiritual agents from the very headquarters of evil" (Ephesians 6:12, Phillips). Literally, the petition from Jesus' model prayer is, "deliver us from the evil one" (Matthew 6:13).

The Christian life is a struggle against the world, the flesh and the devil. To deal with that struggle, growing Christians remember that the Christian life offers divine resources for

Using God's Weapons

the struggle. Contemporary spirituality offers resources for the struggle of life such as meditation techniques, positive visualizing, support groups, assertiveness training, insight, knowledge, education, technology, better diet, exercise. Some of these aren't bad. They just aren't enough.

In Ephesians 6, what we're told to "put on" is "the full armor of God," (Ephesians 6:11) so we may deal effectively with this struggle. At this point in his life, Paul may well have been imprisoned, chained to a Roman soldier. He was also well-versed in the Old Testament, where some of his soldier word pictures come from. Dress like a soldier, says Paul, for the Christian life is a battle. He specifies seven pieces of such a soldier's armor. Let me summarize them in two broad categories:

(1) *Fill your mind with the right stuff!*

The urgent exhortation is to watch how you think. Effectiveness or failure in the Christian struggle often begins in our thoughts.

Put on truth like a soldier's belt.

Protect your thought life (helmet) with the assurance of salvation.

Use the Word of God and prayer, also resources in our thinking.

A battle is going on for the minds of Christian men and women today. Will our view of life be dominated by "the world, the flesh and the devil"? Or will our minds be saturated with the truth of God, the assurance of salvation and the Word of God and prayer?

(2) *Watch the way you live.*

Suit up with righteousness, says Paul. That is, live out your right-relatedness to God through upright actions and behaviors which are in accord with this relationship with God.

Use trust in what God has done for us in Jesus as a

89

Spirituality in a Mixed-Up Age

shield, defending against anything the enemy can throw at you.

Put on "shoes for good news," the gospel of Jesus, which gives peace. Good news is not just for standing still, but for walking, for taking to others. As I am involved in communicating that good news to others, I am wearing armor that empowers me to be victorious in the struggle.

It is in the midst of the struggle of Christian living, not in escape from struggle, that Christians grow. There is no way out of our struggle against the world, the flesh and the devil, just as there is no way out of facing the difficulties of life. But we can be victorious in the struggle when we use the resources of God.

Authentic Christian spirituality is realistic. It faces life with its struggle head-on. It faces the enemies of Christian growth head-on. It doesn't become preoccupied with problems or with the devil. It isn't satisfied with a morose putting up with trouble or with merely grinning and bearing it.

The spirituality of the growing Christian finds joy in the midst of struggle. Julian of Norwich, English mystic of about 1400, is said to have commented about the devil that he may never do as ill as he would, for his might is all locked in God's hand. Therefore, she suggested, God scorns and laughs at the devil and we should do the same. We can laugh at our adversary. We can have joy in the midst of victorious struggle.

Spirituality and the Holy Spirit

(Meditations on Romans 8)

12

No Condemnation

Uniquely Christian spirituality is the work of the Holy Spirit. As we've already seen, Christian spirituality is not just spirituality with a small s, referring merely to the human spirit and its well-being. Rather, it is Spirituality with a capital S, speaking of the Holy Spirit's work in the human spirit.

The Apostle Paul wrote to the Roman Christians: "If anyone does not have the Spirit of Christ, he does not belong to Christ" (Romans 8:9). In other words, the distinguishing characteristic that sets the true Christian apart from the unbelieving person is that the Holy Spirit lives within.

Anglican clergyman and paraphraser of Scripture, J.B. Phillips, put it this way: "Every time we say 'I believe in the Holy Spirit,' we mean that we believe there is a living God able and willing to enter human personality and change it."[1] Understanding the work of the Holy Spirit is thus an important key to making sense of Christian spirituality in an age of half-truths and even outrageous untruths on the subject.

Few passages of Scripture highlight the work of the Holy Spirit more magnificently than does Romans 8. Follow me as we explore together the theme of Christian spirituality found in this great chapter.

Spirituality in a Mixed-Up Age

No Condemnation!

The affirmation, "No condemnation!" captures the joyful theme of the opening verses of Romans 8.

I saw a cartoon strip depicting a pastor talking with a couple who were checking out his church. He speaks to them of his church's approach as "12-Step Christianity." "Basically," he says "we're all recovering sinners. My ministry is about overcoming denial. It's about recommitment, about redemption."

"Wait a minute," the woman inquirer chimes in. "Sinners? Redemption? Doesn't all that imply guilt ... We're looking for a church that's supportive, a place where we can feel good about ourselves. I'm not sure the guilt thing works for us."

"There's so much negativity in the world as it is," says her husband. "On the other hand," he says glancing at the church's brochure, "you do offer racquetball."

"So did the Unitarians, honey," says his wife. "Let's shop around some more."

Guilt isn't cool these days. We'd rather point out how other people are responsible for what we do than face up to what we have done. The New Age movement has a woefully inadequate understanding of sin and guilt, of forgiveness and salvation.

Today, we've also understandably reacted to heavy-handed guilt trip tactics used in some Christian groups. Somewhere I heard the potent line, "Guilt is what neurotic leaders use to keep neurotic followers in line." A "toxic emotion" is what guilt feelings have been called. And for many people, guilt becomes just that.

Where does the Bible stand on "the guilt thing," as the cartoon character put it? Is there a biblical and wholesome spirituality which acknowledges the value of guilt when one has done wrong? Is there a spirituality, which sees guilt as a kind of

94

No Condemnation

alarm bell warning of danger, or a pain that gives evidence of disease? On the other hand, is there a biblical spirituality that also shows us why and how we don't need to live with those alarm bells always ringing and with the incessant pain of guilty consciences?

"No condemnation!" is the way Paul opens Romans 8. Notice, he doesn't say "No guilt!" Paul was a Hebrew. He knew well the elaborate provision in the law of Moses for dealing with sin and its resulting guilt. Paul had also gone to great pains in the first half of this letter to point out how guilty human beings are when we stand before God. "All have sinned and fall short of the glory of God," (Romans 3:23) is one well-known statement. In Romans 7, Paul describes the struggle between what we know to be right and what we find ourselves pulled to do.

While Paul doesn't exclaim, "No guilt!" he does offer "No condemnation!" It is to those who live in relationship with Jesus Christ and experience the work of the Holy Spirit in their lives that this life of no condemnation is possible.

The condemnation Paul highlights is more than just feelings of guilt or even a legal sentence of guilty. The apostle is speaking of a kind of punishment that comes from being guilty. It's like a prison sentence. Condemnation is living with punishment for what we've done. Condemnation is, to use Eugene Peterson's paraphrase of this passage, living "under a continuous, low-lying, black cloud" (*The Message*).

Yes, we have done things which are wrong. Yes, there are times when we may have good reason to feel guilty. But authentic Christian spirituality involves standing before God without an ongoing load of guilt, without a sense of separation from a holy God, and without the feelings of being guilty that destroy our emotional life and our relationships.

In the Greek text of Romans 8, the very first emphatic

Spirituality in a Mixed-Up Age

word is "no." It's as if the apostle were exclaiming, "No condemnation, not a hint, absolutely none."

That's the way it should be. But that's not always the way it is. I know people who have confessed and confessed and asked forgiveness time and time again, but yet have felt no relief from the sense of condemnation. Life is lived under that "low-lying, black cloud." Some people feel they've done something so bad as to make forgiveness impossible. Some can't seem to accept God's forgiveness and then forgive themselves. Some have to live with the consequences of destructive decisions that remind them continuously of what they have done. Some people have a tendency to feel guilty whether they've done anything wrong or not. The feeling of shame is second nature to them. Many people listen to the voice of Satan, one of whose biblical titles is "accuser of our brothers" (Revelation 12:10). It is the devil's business to get Christians to forget, ignore or minimize what Jesus has done for us.

To such people comes the ringing word from Romans 8: No condemnation to those who live in relationship with Jesus. No need to live under a "low-lying, black cloud."

One Friday morning a well-dressed man walked into my church office and asked to speak to a pastor. Not being sure why he had come, I waited for him to state his need. After slowly working up to this point, he finally asked if I had heard of the Cosa Nostra. He was, he told me, a Cosa Nostra soldier. Since his youth, he'd been taught how to kill. He told me that he had done many bad things. However, he had come to faith in Christ through a woman with whom he'd fallen in love, but who had recently died of cancer. His newfound Christian faith made living as a mob soldier very difficult. Right then, he was in big trouble because he had struggled with doing what mob leaders had assigned him.

No Condemnation

Even as we spoke he was a hunted man. I was able to pray with him and affirm that God had forgiven him, and with God there was no condemnation. Now, he has to face his years in the Cosa Nostra, from which there is no easy exit. I don't know whether or not he has been successful in extricating himself from the mob's clutches. I do know that with the Cosa Nostra, there was and is condemnation. But with God, there is "no condemnation!"

And why? What is the reason for this ringing declaration?

Paul gives us two reasons for this great affirmation. They are reasons which point to the essence of Christian spirituality.

There is no condemnation, first, *because of what Jesus has done.*

"There is therefore no condemnation." When you come to a "therefore" in the Bible, you look to see what it's there for. This "therefore" harks back to all the Apostle Paul has said in the first seven rich, content-packed chapters of this letter. We might summarize it this way: People need God and are dependent on what Jesus has done for them.

Paul moves on in verse 3 to picture Jesus as a "sin offering." The law of Moses prescribed offerings of animals to take care of guilt when people broke God's law and offended God's holiness. The New Testament tells us that what Jesus did on the cross is like those Old Testament offerings. Jesus' offering of Himself atones for or covers over our sin so that it is no longer a barrier to relationship with a holy God. "God did by sending his own son in the likeness of sinful man to be a sin offering" (Romans 8:3). In other words, we stand before God without condemnation, not because of what we have or have not done, but solely because of what Jesus has done for us.

Spirituality in a Mixed-Up Age

One more phrase speaks of what Jesus is and Jesus has done for us. "No condemnation," exclaimed Paul, "for those who are in Christ Jesus." The apostle had a magnificent obsession that crops up again and again in his letters. It was this theme of being "in Christ." It was relationship with Jesus, but a specific kind of relationship. Union with Jesus, oneness with Jesus is what it was. I am in Him, He in me. "In Christ!"

In that oneness, we become something more than we were otherwise. A bar of iron is cold, dull, hard. Let that bar of iron be placed in the fire. It becomes a glowing, flexible, useful piece of metal. The iron doesn't cease to be iron. The fire doesn't cease to be fire. But iron in union with fire becomes something different, something more useful. There is no condemnation for that person who is so united with Jesus that he or she is actually more of a person than before.

No condemnation! Why? Because of what Jesus has done for us.

Paul gives us his second reason for no condemnation — *because of what the Holy Spirit does.*

According to Romans 8, *the Holy Spirit liberates us.*

Human beings are in bondage to the urges and drives of self-centeredness. It's amazing how much of one's life and behavior arises out of self-centeredness.

One of the individuals investigated for involvement in the bombing of the Oklahoma City federal building was known to be extremely antigovernment. He even wrote to his county authorities declaring he was no longer a citizen. Yet, during that period of about six years, he is thought to have received some $90,000 in agricultural subsidy payments from that same government. Political rhetoric meant little when it came to money in his pocket.

Human beings are in bondage to self-centeredness.

No Condemnation

Though we know we should do better, we can't seem to pull it off by ourselves. Have you noticed that? This is what the Apostle Paul calls "the law of sin and death" (verse 2). But through the Spirit of life, says Paul, I am freed from this bondage. "Sin shall not be your master," is the way he puts it in Romans 6:14.

The Holy Spirit also *empowers us*. Those united with Jesus Christ live according to the Spirit, says Paul. Instead of self-centeredness, the Holy Spirit is the dominating influence of our lives. In Romans 8:9, the apostle declares, "You ... are controlled not by the sinful nature but by the Spirit, if the Spirit of God lives in you ..."

We have a source of life and power outside ourselves. What we are and what we accomplish is not due simply to our own best efforts, but to what God's Spirit does in us. I like the way *The Message* paraphrases Paul: "What the law code asked for but we couldn't deliver is accomplished as we, instead of redoubling our own efforts, simply embrace what the Spirit is doing in us." The Holy Spirit liberates and empowers us. The Holy Spirit is God at work in us. That's why we don't have to face life under a "low-lying black cloud" of condemnation, shame, self-reproach.

Some people today opt for a spirituality that ignores the reality and validity of guilt. Like the cartoon couple, they're not comfortable with guilt. That's attempting spirituality without reality. And what's the point in that?

Others have caught sight of their guilt but have become preoccupied with it, focusing on it, living in bondage to it. Their lives are lived under the black cloud of condemnation. And a black cloud spirituality is no more wholesome than a spirituality without reality.

The key is to see that yes, we do need what Jesus has

Spirituality in a Mixed-Up Age

done to deal with our guilt. And yes, we do need the Holy Spirit in our lives to be liberated and empowered people. It's that kind of vision that lifts this "low-lying, black cloud." It's that kind of vision that makes possible a spirituality of no condemnation.

13

Belonging

When my children were small, we would occasionally have a houseful of kids, our own plus their friends. A neighbor or saleperson would stop by. "Are these all your children?" they would ask. My wife and I would quickly point out who were ours and who were not.

There's a difference between children who belong and children who visit. Neighborhood children would call me by name, or maybe Mr. Abbott, or Pastor Abbott. My children would call me Dad. If somebody got hurt, my children would come crying to me or their mother, while neighborhood kids would go off to their parents. There is a difference between kids who belong and kids who are visiting.

Belonging involves loving relationship. Belonging involves trusting security. Belonging involves a sense of identity. Everybody needs to belong to somebody.

An important part of who we are comes from who we belong to and who belongs to us. The quest to belong can motivate destructive behavior. Young persons join street gangs; people engage in promiscuous sex; seekers become part of a religious cult. These are self-destructive behaviors often motivated by the desire to belong.

"Who We Are" is a chapter in a book by Henri Nouwen, entitled *Here and Now*. In it, this perceptive Roman Catholic priest points out that we usually give one of three answers to the

101

Spirituality in a Mixed-Up Age

question, Who are we? We often say:
- We are what we do, or
- We are what others say about us, or
- We are what we have.

In other words, we are our success, we are our popularity, we are our power. But those are false identities, says Nouwen. Jesus came to tell us "You are not what the world makes you; you are children of God." Writes Nouwen, "The spiritual life requires a constant claiming of our true identity. Our true identity is that we are God's children, the beloved sons and daughters of our heavenly Father."[1]

True Christian spirituality is refusing to let our identity depend upon external and this world-imposed factors, but, rather, on the reality that we are God's beloved because of Christ.

When the Apostle Paul writes to the Romans about the role of the Holy Spirit in believers, he speaks of fostering a sense of belonging to God. An important function of the Holy Spirit is to make clear to us that we belong to God and we belong to one another in the believing community. Romans 8:15-17 eloquently expresses this theme of belonging. I see Paul painting at least three word pictures, each of them speaking to this core issue of spirituality, belonging to God.

The first word picture is that of adoption. In Paul's world, a couple without a male heir might adopt a son who would then perpetuate the family name and inherit the family estate. That child would be just as much a child of the adoptive parents as a biological child. The adopted child did not belong to the family originally. He was very likely an orphan or a slave. But through the choice of the father, this child became part of his family and really belonged.

Belonging

The apostle writes, "You did not receive a spirit that makes you a slave again to fear, but you received the Spirit of sonship." Paul literally wrote "the Spirit of adoption." Christians are not to be filled with the spirit of fear, which comes from not belonging, but rather the Holy Spirit of adoption, who assures us that we do belong to God.

Christians are all adopted children who at one time were orphans in this world. Scripture speaks of us as without God, lost, alone. But because of His great and undeserved love, God reaches out to us and makes a place for us in His family so that we belong to Him.

In the society within which the early church grew, unwanted children were often simply abandoned, left on doorsteps at night. Bands of Christians would go up and down city streets in the morning picking up these unwanted, discarded babies who didn't belong. These orphaned infants would be taken to Christian wet nurses in the city plaza who would care for their needs. They would then be incorporated into the family of God, belonging to God and to the church. The church grew by picking up the unwanted of the world, wrapping the arms of Jesus' love around them, enabling them to belong to the family of God. That's adoption!

When we're adopted into the family, we can call God by His intimate name, Abba, Father. This is a word from Aramaic, Jesus' language. It is used today in Hebrew speaking families as a familiar term by which children address their father. "Dad, Pops, Poppa." While this word was used to address human fathers, nowhere in all Jewish literature outside the New Testament is this word ever used to address God, the Heavenly Father. It would have been unthinkable for an Old Testament Jew to address God in this manner. Apparently, however, the disciples heard Jesus use this term when He spoke to God. They,

Spirituality in a Mixed-Up Age

then, adopted Jesus' revolutionary pattern of calling God "Dad."

Fifteenth-century reformer Martin Luther wrote of the little word Abba, "This is but a little word, and yet notwithstanding it comprehendeth all things ... Although I be oppressed with anguish and terror on every side, and seem to be forsaken and utterly cast away from thy presence, yet am I thy child, and thou art my Father for Christ's sake: I am beloved because of the Beloved."2

The picture is adoption. The outcome is secure identity as God's children. This is what the Holy Spirit makes possible in us. This is authentic Christian spirituality.

The second word picture of belonging in these Romans 8 verses is that of the *inner voice*. You've heard people talk about a little voice inside them. Sometimes we wonder about what that voice apparently tells them to do. We may be a little suspicious of inner voices. But this is the picture Paul paints. "The Spirit himself testifies with our spirit that we are God's children" (Romans 8:16).

My own spirit has a voice. It says to me, "You have indeed responded to God's invitation to be His. You have turned away from what separates you from God. You do belong to God."

I also hear the inner voice of God's Spirit. That voice of the Holy Spirit gives witness with the voice of my own spirit and confirms that I am, indeed, a child of God. "God's Spirit touches our spirits and confirms who we really are. We know who he is, and we know who we are: Father and children" (*The Message*).

One of John Wesley's great themes was what he called "the witness of the Spirit." By this, Wesley meant assurance of salvation, of sins forgiven, of belonging to God. As with most of his preaching, this emphasis came out of Wesley's own experi-

Belonging

ence. As a young man, John desperately sought salvation and assurance of this salvation through ceaseless involvement in good works.

One author writes about him, "As a merciless taskmaster, he drove himself in all the religious disciplines and services that could be imagined. He got up at 4 a.m. to pray and study. He met with like-minded men to form what was called the "Holy Club." He visited people in prison. Above what was absolutely necessary to live on, he gave his money away. He was neurotically anxious about his use of time.

He went as a missionary to Indians in the colony of Georgia. On board ship to America, Wesley came in contact with German Moravians, Christians who seemed to have peace and assurance. During a storm at sea they sang and prayed together, giving evidence of what they called the assurance of salvation. In Georgia, Wesley met a Moravian pastor who asked him, "Does the Spirit of God bear witness with your spirit that you are a child of God?" This ordained Anglican priest didn't know how to answer. "Do you know that Jesus has saved you?" pressed the missionary. Wesley could only reply: "I *hope* He has died to save me."

It was not until he had returned from Georgia, a failure as a missionary, that Wesley experienced that assurance of salvation for which he sought. On May 24, 1738, he worshiped in a little Moravian meeting house on Aldersgate Street in London. As a layleader read from Luther's preface to the Epistle to the Romans, John Wesley said, "I felt my heart strangely warmed ... and an assurance was given me that he had taken away my sins, even mine ..."

Wesley then preached that this inner voice of God's Spirit, assuring us that we belong to God, is the "common privilege of Christians." As he preached on the Romans 8 text, he

105

Spirituality in a Mixed-Up Age

said, "The testimony of the Spirit is an inward impression on the soul, whereby the Spirit of God directly witnesses to my spirit that I am a child of God; that Jesus Christ hath loved me, and given himself for me; and that all my sins are blotted out, and I, even I, am reconciled to God. Spirituality in the Wesleyan tradition emphasizes the importance of this inner voice.

Do we know that we belong? Do we live with assurance that, regardless of who we are or what we've done we belong to God through Jesus? That's the privilege of all who believe in Christ for their salvation. It is that confidence which enabled blind gospel songwriter Fanny Crosby to sing:

Blessed Assurance, Jesus is mine.
O what a foretaste of glory divine.
Heir of salvation, purchase of God.
Born of His Spirit, washed in His blood.

A final Pauline picture of belonging is that of an *inheritance*.

"Now, if we are children, then we are heirs — heirs of God and co-heirs with Christ ..." Because Christians are joint heirs with Christ, our inheritance is the same as that of Jesus. After suffering on earth, Jesus returned to the glory He had with the Father before the world began. Christians, as co-heirs with Jesus, share His sufferings and share His glory. We will not only see His glory, but also share in it. This is our hope and expectation! Regardless of what is going on now in our lives we have this to look forward to!

A young woman adopted into the beautiful home of a high-ranking business executive, said, "Isn't it wonderful that I share in all the beautiful things Daddy provides just as much as my sister who was born to these things?"

The Holy Spirit speaks clearly to us, "You are God's

Belonging

beloved." You belong to God. And not only that, you belong to the body, the community of believers. Paul wrote to the Romans (12:5), "In Christ we who are many form one body, and each member belongs to all the others." Though we may not feel like we belong some of the time, reality is more than feeling. And the reality is that we do belong to God and to each other. This is authentic Christian spirituality.

14

Help for Hang-ups

Contemporary American society is extremely aware of hang-ups. While older dictionaries didn't even contain the word "hang-up," more recent versions include the term, defining it as preoccupation, fixation, psychological block.

According to some authorities, as many as 15 percent of Americans suffer from some major mental/emotional disorder at any given time. In addition, one in three Americans suffer from a serious mental illness sometime during their lives. There are half a million support groups attended weekly by some 15 million Americans, according to some estimates. In fact, it's almost fashionable to be in recovery from something.

So what are our hang-ups? Can we name them? Inferiority complex, codependency, addiction of one kind or another, anger and its manifestations, depression? Maybe you don't like your parents. Maybe you can't stand authority figures. Maybe you don't like yourself.

And what do we want God to do with our hang-ups? Do we think God should just snap His finger and get rid of them for us? A college-age woman with a drinking problem once screamed at me, "Why didn't God just take the bottle out of my hand?"

These days, many understand salvation primarily as therapy for hang-ups. Ministry is often seen as therapy. The

109

Spirituality in a Mixed-Up Age

church is here to provide therapy. God is little more than a cosmic therapist.

Spirituality today is often seen as that which comes out of therapy. Often popular spirituality is understood merely in feeling terms →it's how I feel when I feel better. But an authentic biblical spirituality is more than pop psychology. God's provision for our emotional and mental weakness may include, but is certainly more than, psychological therapy.

"The Spirit helps us in our weakness," wrote Paul in Romans 8:26. His word for "weakness" can mean infirmity. It's the same word used in Luke's account of a woman "crippled by a spirit," as the *NIV* puts it (Luke 13:11). J.B. Phillips paraphrases her ailment as "from some psychological cause." Maybe it was a series of hang-ups, that had taken their toll on her physical body, creating a bent-over condition.

The Holy Spirit promotes wholeness in Christians. Holiness, if properly understood, is wholeness. But what God's Spirit does is not so much to give our problems a quick fix as to provide us resources to deal with them.

God's Spirit gives us wholesome ways of thinking. God's Spirit gives us ways of living and behaving and relating to one another, which foster wholeness. But that's not the quick and easy fix looked for by many today. This is not "Six Easy Steps to be Healthy, Wealthy and Wise."

One observer writes about the contemporary spiritual quest of many as "a desire for instant ecstasy, instant salvation ... the quest for the correct method, the right mantra, the shortcut which brings insight ..." That may be pop psychology, but it's not true biblical spirituality.

Paul's specific illustration of the Holy Spirit's response to our need in Romans 8 has to do with weakness in prayer.

Help for Hang-ups

That's important! "The Holy Spirit helps us in our weakness ... The Spirit Himself intercedes for us."

But the principle is even broader than prayer. In all our weaknesses, including our emotional weakness and our hang-ups, the Holy Spirit is available. That does not mean all human weakness can simply be remedied by crying out to the Holy Spirit. There are real physical diseases which often need medicine and/or surgery to heal. Real emotional/mental problems arise which may manifest themselves in physical diseases that often need the response of trained therapists to bring about wholeness. Biblical spirituality doesn't rule out medicine or therapy, but recognizes that the Holy Spirit has a central role in dealing with our weaknesses, our hang-ups. Biblical spirituality sees the Holy Spirit as central in true wholeness.

Romans 8 suggests at least two ways in which the Holy Spirit works with us in our hang-ups. For one thing, *the Holy Spirit gives us hope in hang-ups.*

A natural response in the midst of weakness is discouragement, depression, even despair. When I find myself hung-up on a hang-up, especially when it's for the umpteenth time, I am discouraged. But Paul identifies hope-producing factors in the midst of hang-ups.

The apostle talks about our assurance of future redemption (Romans 8:18-25). Paul talks about the difference between living in this fallen world, distorted by sin as it is, and our confident anticipation of future glory, which is the believer's hope. In this world there is suffering, pain, weakness, hang-ups. Even the world of nature is subject to decay, corruption, death. Even the natural world, distorted from its original intent, is not what God intended. But according to Paul, we look forward to a time of total redemption, a time of complete liberation. These bodies of ours, plagued with physical weakness, as well as these per-

Spirituality in a Mixed-Up Age

sonalities of ours, distressed by emotional hang-ups, will one day be totally redeemed. We will be liberated from weaknesses and hang-ups. Even the effect of sin on the natural creation will be remedied. These are grounds for hope → a hope-producing factor in the midst of hang-ups.

According to verse 23, the presence of the Holy Spirit in our lives now is a kind of guarantee, a down payment on that final redemption to which we look forward. In Ephesians 1, Paul speaks of the Holy Spirit as a "deposit guaranteeing our inheritance until the redemption of those who are God's possession ..." (Ephesians 1:14).

Because of this great assurance, we can regard our experience of present weakness as a transient stage on the way to glory. Present hang-ups, current infirmities, the weaknesses of this life are not eternal. Thank God!

We can identify with the motto a businessman had on his desk. PBPGINTWMY. When asked to explain, he responded, "It means please be patient, God is not through with me yet!"

Some of us may be less patient with ourselves than God is with us. We browbeat and bully ourselves, wondering how God could possibly love and accept us as we are. But the wonder of God's grace is that in His love and mercy, He does accept us where He finds us and points us in the hope-filled direction of final redemption.

Another hope-filled factor is the availability of present victory. All through Romans 5-8, Paul emphasized that Christians are not simply stuck with a sin-ridden, infirmity-laden personality until that final redemption. God can do something with us even now! There can be at least substantial healing in areas of weakness even now. PBPGINTWMY not only suggests patience with the process, but also the assurance that the pro-

Help for Hang-ups

cess is going on. As I allow Him to work, God is doing something in me through the Holy Spirit.

Paul wrote to the Philippian Christians, "He who began a good work in you will carry it on to completion until the day of Christ Jesus" (Philippians 1:6). Do we believe that?

The Holy Spirit gives us hope in hang-ups. In addition, the Holy Spirit gives us help in our hang-ups. The Holy Spirit can help us in our weakness, whether that weakness is in prayer or in an area of emotional infirmity.

Paul's word translated "help" is a picturesque one. It is the compound of three Greek words translated *with, on the other side*, and *takes hold of*. Put them together and what do you get? The Holy Spirit takes hold with us on the other side. The burden is too heavy for us to carry alone. But the Holy Spirit comes alongside and says, "Friend, I'll help you shoulder that load if you'll let me. I'll take hold on the other side with you. I'll help you."

As a boy growing up in India, where my parents were missionaries, I remember seeing shoulder-height, stone platforms beside the road. When a man or woman with a heavy load — probably carried on the head or shoulder — needed rest, the traveler stopped at one of these platforms, pushed the load over on it and enjoyed relief.

"I heard the voice of Jesus say, 'Come unto me and rest;
Lay down, O weary one, lay down your head upon my breast.'
I came to Jesus as I was, weary and worn, and sad;
I found in him a resting place, and he has made me glad."

The Holy Spirit is the rest-giving One, the Spirit of Jesus, Who understands us because He was one of us. It is this Spirit of Jesus Who helps us in our weakness.

Spirituality in a Mixed-Up Age

An authentic Christian spirituality is hope-filled because of the Holy Spirit. It draws on the help-giving resources of the same Spirit. Spiritual people recognize their hang-ups but are not victimized by them or deterred from living fully and in wholenesss. We do not demand of the Spirit a quick fix or an immediate cure. Rather, we commit to a life of hope and help in our hang-ups through the indwelling of the Holy Spirit.

15

Good From Everything

One of our church couples served as a volunteer host family for a man from South Carolina, who was having a bone marrow transplant here in Seattle. The sick man and his wife worshiped with us. We had public prayer for healing on his behalf. I had the privilege of visiting these Christians at the hospital. He was a farmer, strong and healthy as can be. Even though there was no cancer in his family, out of the blue, leukemia struck. They had to leave their farm in the hands of their kids, pack up, and come to Seattle for months of treatment. But they expressed no complaint or self pity. In them, I found the conviction that God was bringing good from this crisis.

One Sunday evening as I was visiting, a nurse came into the room. David showed her cards received from the bone marrow donor. This donor was also a Christian. She had a sense of mission about giving her bone marrow and was praying for the one who would receive it. As the nurse read these encouraging cards, she was moved. There was blessing coming from the hospital room not doom and gloom. There was good coming even from this adversity.

Situations arise in most of our lives which have not turned out as we intended or hoped. There may be uncertainty as to why some things have happened. But there need never be loss of hope. For out of the most trying circumstances, God can

Spirituality in a Mixed-Up Age

bring good. Authentic Christian spirituality believes God can bring good from anything and everything.

But it's not always good on our terms. It's not necessarily a good which is convenient and makes us comfortable. It is good according to God's purposes, God's plan.

Romans 8:28 is one of the most often-quoted verses in the Bible. But it's often quoted tritely and with an inadequate understanding of its meaning. The *King James Version* translation is, "All things work together for good to them that love God," which has been understood to mean:

"Everything's going to turn out all right," or
"Everything will come out in the wash," or
"Don't worry, be happy, things will get better, you'll see! Every cloud has a silver lining!"

There is a sense in which we can find some good in everything that happens, even those things which seem to be bad. And spiritual people are those who look for the good in everything. But that's not the real focus of Romans 8:28.

It is not so much that "all things work together for good," but rather *in all things God is working according to His good purposes for those who love Him.*

To understand Romans 8:28, we need to check out verse 29. From this verse, we understand *God's Purpose.*

Is it God's purpose that you and I be happy?
Is it God's purpose that you and I be at ease or comfortable?
Is it God's purpose that you and I have fun?

According to the Apostle Paul, God's ultimate purpose for us is that we become like Jesus. "Conformed to the likeness of His Son." That's the word in verse 29. What a difference that perspective makes in how we understand Romans 8:28!

But probe a little deeper into this purpose of God.

Good From Everything

There are three words either in these verses in Romans or implied by them.

One word is *transformation*. The word translated "conformed" in verse 29 is the root of our English word "metamorphosis," meaning to undergo a profound change of form or structure. When a caterpillar, through a chrysalis, becomes a butterfly, metamorphosis has occurred. When Eliza Dolittle, in *My Fair Lady*, is transformed from flower seller to princess, metamorphosis has occurred. When a self-centered human being becomes a Christ-centered and Christlike human being, metamorphosis or transformation has occurred. That's God's purpose!

In addition to transformation, another word appears here in Romans 8 about which thorny theological debates have swirled for centuries. It is the word *predestination*. "Those God foreknew he also predestined to be conformed to the likeness of his Son ..." (verse 29).

Historically, some have claimed that God irresistably chooses some and not others for salvation, that His choice has nothing at all to do with our own desires or will. This has left some to wonder about whether or not they were among the predestined.

There is mystery in the whole subject of predestination, which makes it difficult to define where God's purpose ends and where human freedom begins. Maybe that's as God intends. But what the Bible teaches about the purpose of God neither eliminates human freedom nor eliminates the importance of our free response to God.

What is emphasized here in Romans 8 is that God has ordained a plan of salvation for human beings and a plan for making men and women like Jesus. It is God's unalterable purpose that those who respond to Jesus should become like Him.

Spirituality in a Mixed-Up Age

In addition to transformation and predestination, there is creation. God's purpose is to create for Himself nothing less than a body, a family, a people who will bear the family likeness and for whom Jesus will be the firstborn, the oldest brother.

It is God's purpose to create a family of people who are vitally related to Jesus Christ, the older brother, and who reflect the family likeness. St. Augustine once said: "What else can save us but your hand remaking what you have made?"

It is through transformation, predestination and new creation that God works out His purpose. From eternity past to eternity future, this is what God is working on. From God's original intention in creating human beings in the Garden of Eden to His plan in sending Jesus to the world, to His ultimate intention of glorifying those whom He has redeemed. This is God's unchanging purpose, a purpose which controls our understanding of Romans 8:28.

Having observed God's purpose, think also about God's process.

The process of God's working with you and me is guided by this purpose. It is to this purpose that God is working in and through everything that comes into our lives. It is not just to make us happy, comfortable, respectable and at ease. It is not just to satisfy our own wants and wishes. Rather, it is to make us like Jesus. God sets such high priority on our conformity to Jesus that He wants to use everything that comes into our lives to accomplish that purpose.

God may not directly send all things to us. Things may come our way because we live in a fallen world in which there is accident, disease and tragedy; or because someone around us has behaved foolishly, or we ourselves have made foolish choices. But God wants to use all of those things, even foolish things we have done, in the process of making us like Jesus.

Good From Everything

And who is God's instrument in this process?
It is the Holy Spirit. In the verses before Romans 8:28, Paul has just been talking about the work of the Holy Spirit, how the Spirit helps us in our weakness, and about how the Spirit helps us in our inadequacy in prayer. It is the same Spirit Who is at work in the lives of those who love God to accomplish this great purpose. It is the Holy Spirit at work in this great process.

But What is Our Part?

God's purpose through His Spirit is to make us increasingly like Jesus. What part do we have to play in this process?
For one thing, we are to love God. "In all things God works for the good of those who love Him." When we love God, we want what God wants more than anything else. Self-centered concerns take a backseat to the overriding purposes of God.
St. Augustine used to say, "Love God and do as you please." What did he mean? When we love God, we will do what pleases God.
But further, we are to look at Jesus. We become what we look at. We become like that which preoccupies our minds and hearts.
The story is told of a boy named Ernest, who would look longingly at the great stone face on the side of a mountain near his village. It was a strong, kind, honorable face that thrilled the heart of this boy. There was a legend that some day a man would appear who would look like the great stone face. Throughout his childhood, and even after he became a man, Ernest kept looking at the great face and for the man who was like it. One day, when the villagers were discussing the legend, someone suddenly cried out, "Behold, Ernest is himself the likeness of the great stone face." Indeed he was! He had become like what he looked at.

Spirituality in a Mixed-Up Age

Our part is to love God, look at Jesus and live life from this perspective. It's not just what happens to us that counts. It's how we respond to what happens to us that makes the difference. It's whether or not we allow God's Spirit to work through what happens that makes the difference.

Do we see everything as an opportunity for God's Spirit to be at work in us, making us more like Jesus? Do we really believe that God's Spirit can work in all things to make us and mold us into the image of Jesus? Do we live life from this perspective? This is truly living out Romans 8:28. This is authentic Christian spirituality.

16

Spiritual Music

My family recently gave me a compact disc player. Along with it came a compact disc of Beethoven's Ninth Symphony, that marvelously strong piece with the climaxing choral section from which we get our tune to the hymn "Joyful, Joyful, We Adore Thee." I listened as the symphony built to a climax, and then to another climax, and another. Like midwestern thunder rolling across the plains, there is one crescendo climax after another. As I sat in a darkened living room listening, I thought: *"Wow! That's like Romans 8!"*

The spiritual music of this great chapter begins with the liberating affirmation, "No condemnation for those who are in Christ Jesus." We hear Paul sing of the assurance of belonging to God which the Holy Spirit makes possible. We listen as Paul's music deals with how the Holy Spirit provides both hope and help in human hang-ups. We hear the music soar as Paul develops his great theme that in all the circumstances of life, God wants to work through His Spirit to make Christians more and more like Jesus.

At the end of Romans 8:31 you sense a pause in the music. In Paul's dictation of Romans to his scribe it may have been a long pause. I see the intense apostle pacing up and down, thinking, muttering to himself. I see the waiting scribe, poised with pen in hand. "What then, shall we say in response

121

Spirituality in a Mixed-Up Age

to this?" says Paul finally, with a kind of dramatic formula he has already used in Chapters 6 and 7. "What shall we say ... to this?" I hear him repeating the question as he meditates on the fantastic implications of what he has already said.

There's another pause. Then, when Paul resumes his dictation, it is not carefully reasoned prose which flows from his mouth. It is oratory, poetry, great music. A series of fervent questions builds the music of these last verses of Romans 8 to their exciting conclusion. It's something like the climax of a great symphony, or like the finale of a contemporary Christian song, or even like the climaxing windup of a rock song.

This is the "music of the Spirit," the song which the Holy Spirit can bring to human hearts. This is the crescendo to what Paul has been saying about the work of God's Spirit in human lives. Now the music of the Spirit can be quiet, gentle, even sad at times. But when people have God's Spirit at work in them, the music, at least some of the time →maybe most of time — ought to soar and crescendo triumphantly.

We are often unexcited about what God does for us through Jesus and the Holy Spirit. Someone passed on to me a new slant on the Sermon on the Mount, patterned after the responses of many contemporary students. After the great words of the Beatitudes, this version has Simon Peter saying, "Are we supposed to know this stuff?"

    Andrew said, "Do we have to write this down?"
    James said, "Will we have a test on this?"
    Philip said, "I don't have any paper."
    Bartholomew said, "Do we have to turn this in?"
    Matthew said, "Can I go to the bathroom?"
    Judas said, "What does this have to do with real life?"
    Jesus wept!
Of course, students aren't the only ones who tend to re-

Spiritual Music

duce great themes to the ordinary, mundane and unexciting.

If there really is no condemnation to those who are in Christ; and if we really do belong to God, and by the Spirit are enabled to call God "Abba, Father"; and if the Holy Spirit does help us in our weaknesses and human hang-ups; and if in every circumstance of life, God's Spirit is at work to make us more like Jesus — then the music of the Spirit should build to some marvelously triumphant climaxes.

The spiritual music of Romans 8 comes to a climax in a series of rhetorical questions to which the answer is obvious. Paul asks the question only to affirm the great truths he believes and which motivate his overflowing music.

The first crescendo question is about *God's triumph in us*. "If God is for us, who can be against us?" (verse 31).

There may be many enemies against us. But if God is for us, or if God is on our side, then those enemies need not triumph over us. Those enemies may seem to triumph, even kill the believer as they did the Apostle Paul himself in the very city to whose Christians he was writing. According to tradition, both the apostles Paul and Peter were martyred in Rome. But even the death of these leaders did not destroy the young church. In fact, it was said in the early church that "the blood of the martyrs has become the seed of the church."

After Martin Luther's courageous affirmations of gospel truth had stirred up opposition to him, he was summoned to appear before the parliament of the Holy Roman Empire, which was meeting in the German city of Worms. Luther left his hometown of Wittenberg, believing he had been summoned to his death. His friends urged him to go into hiding on the way to Worms. But he declared he would go on even if there were as many devils in Worms as tiles on the housetops. On April 16, 1521, Luther arrived in Worms and made his way through

123

Spirituality in a Mixed-Up Age

dense crowds of people to the site of the meeting. He looked around at those who would be his judges, clearly recognizing their opposition to what he stood for. Yet he exclaimed, "God is for me."

For two days, Luther appeared before parliament and the emperor who condemned him as a heretic, giving him 21 days to recant or face arrest and prosecution. On his way back home Luther was kidnapped by friends and kept in safekeeping for a time at the Wartburg castle. There, Luther wrote his hymn well-known by its opening line, "A mighty fortress is our God ..." Luther sang what Paul also knew, "If God is for us, who can be against us?"

The second crescendo question with which Paul's spiritual music soars is about *God's gifts to us*. "He who did not hesitate to spare his own Son but gave him up for us all – how will he not also, along with him, graciously give us all things?" (verse 32). J.B. Phillips paraphrases it this way: "He who did not grudge his own Son but gave him up for us all – can we not trust such a God to give us, with him, everything else that we can need?" If God gave us Jesus, how will He not give us anything else we need and anything else that is for our good?

Christian gospel is not so much about a demanding God as about a generous God.

- A God Who created the heavens and earth and all that is in them and gave this glorious creation as a kind of love gift to human beings;
- A God Who gave us His only Son Who would be the means by which we could be in friendship with God once more;
- A God Who forgives our sins;
- A God Who pours out the gift of the Holy Spirit upon those who believe;

Spiritual Music

🔘 A God Who showers us with grace-gifts of the Spirit so we may serve Him effectively.

This is a giving God, a generous God. The music of the Spirit crescendoes and soars with thanks and praise for God's good gifts.

This spiritual music now crescendoes with a third question. It's actually the combination of two questions, both of which sing of God's salvation. "Who will bring any charge against those whom God has chosen?" (verse 33). And, "Who is he that condemns?" (verse 34).

These questions call to mind the image of a law court familiar to most Americans. But the trial Paul envisions is a remarkable one. It's not trial by jury but by judge. The divine judge, in Paul's mind, has already pronounced a verdict of acquittal, acquitted not because we have done nothing wrong — we have — but acquitted because Jesus, the attorney for the defense, intercedes on our behalf.

It's like a trial that opens with the verdict of acquittal. The prosecution brings a charge against us, but it's unacceptable to the judge, and we are acquitted. The prosecution tries again with another charge. But again it's thrown out. We are acquitted! Again and again the prosecution tries to charge and condemn us without success. We have been acquitted before the divine court of God because of Jesus and what He did for us on the cross.

One can carry the law court image too far. Salvation is more than a legal declaration of acquittal before God. Salvation is the healing of our wounds and our sickness, and the restoration of friendship and covenant relationship with God. But salvation is also acquittal, that is, freedom from a guilty conscience, nagging guilt and condemnation.

This is something to sing about! Christians through the

Spirituality in a Mixed-Up Age

generations have done just that. Whenever and wherever there has been a new celebration of God's great gift of salvation, there has been an outburst of singing.

"O for a thousand tongues to sing
My great Redeemer's praise ...
"O that with yonder sacred throng,
We at His feet may fall.
We'll join the everlasting song,
And crown him Lord of all."
"I will sing of my Redeemer and His wondrous love to me;
On the cruel cross he suffered from the curse to set me free.
Sing, O sing of my Redeemer, with His blood He purchased me ... "

And there's more that we sing!

This is the music of the Spirit, the crescendo which has sung about God's triumph through us, God's gifts to us, and God's salvation for us. The music swells and grows in intensity once more with a final affirmation hidden in one more question, "Who shall separate us from the love of Christ?" (verse 35). This is the question of *our security*.

Remember, Paul was writing to Christians whose lives within a few short years would be disrupted by great anti-Christian persecution under the Emperor Nero. Christians would be blamed for the fire that gutted Rome. Christians would be cast to wild animals in the Roman coliseum. Christian leaders like Paul would meet their death. But even in such calamities, Christians could know the security of relationship with God through Christ.

While many Christians believe their salvation to be unconditionally secure, others have gotten the idea that theirs

Spiritual Music

hangs by a tenuous thread. If they don't love God enough, serve God sufficiently, obey all the rules, look right, talk right, act right, they will be severed from connection with Christ.

While it is true that the Wesleyan tradition does not believe in an unconditional kind of eternal security, it is also true that it does not teach everlasting insecurity either. We do belong to God. God is our Abba, Father. It is from within this place of security that we grow, serve and confidently live out our faith and make the music of the Spirit.

For nine weeks Dewitt Finley, salesman from Montana, held on to life and faith while in his stranded vehicle high on top of Oregon's southwestern coastal range. Trying to take shortcut forest service roads in the winter, Finley apparently got stuck. He waited for rescue, which never came. He wrote letters on a legal pad that were discovered when he was finally found dead. But during nine weeks of subsisting on melted snow water, Finley never lost faith and trust in God.

He wrote to his boss about God, "He has met my needs daily and I'm alive, well and comforted. I have no control over my life. It's all in His hands," Finley wrote, still hopeful of rescue. "If not, I'll see you in glory. I know God will bless you and yours," he affirmed. Dewitt Finley died secure, trusting in his God.

Hear the spiritual music in this contemporary paraphrase, "Do you think anyone is going to be able to drive a wedge between us and Christ's love for us? There is no way! Not trouble, not hard times, not hatred, not hunger, not homelessness, not bullying threats, not backstabbing ... None of this fazes us because Jesus loves us ... Absolutely *nothing* can get between us and God's love because of the way that Jesus our Master has embraced us" (Romans 8, *The Message*).

That's the security we have in Christ, the music of the

Spirituality in a Mixed-Up Age

Spirit and the celebration of Christians. Do we have that music welling up in our hearts? Yes, I know there are days when the music seems heavy, dreary, sad. But when it's hard to sing our own song, we can join in the community's song, affirming the faith of the gathered congregation of believers.

We sing the music of the Spirit because authentic Christian spirituality is always a singing faith.

To make good sense of spirituality today requires that we live the life of the Spirit. It is the Holy Spirit Who liberates from condemnation, assures us that we belong, gives us hope and help in the midst of our hang-ups and gives us a confident, singing faith.

What is our role? We receive the life of the Spirit, cooperate with the purposes of the Spirit within us and live daily in the power of the Spirit. But it is God's Spirit Who produces the spiritual life. Biblical spirituality is not merely something we develop within ourselves because of insight, knowledge, ethical practices, devotional exercises or even spiritual disciplines. It is the work of God.

Spirituality — The Difference It Makes

17
Stories and Spirituality

I used to be impatient with stories. I used to say, "Oh, that's just a story!" I'm still a little impatient for the punch line when someone tells me a story and takes too long or throws in endless detail.

I've come to see, however, that stories really are important. I've also observed that everyone likes stories. One Sunday, a person's comment on my sermon was, "But you didn't tell any stories today!" Most preachers know that what people often remember of a message is a powerful story.

Whatever else the Bible is, it's a story. "In the beginning, God created ..." – the story of origins. "Once upon a time, there was this man named Abraham ..." – story of the patriarchs and their families. "Then a new king, who did not know about Joseph, came to power in Egypt ..." That's the way the story of the Exodus, the wilderness wanderings, and the promised land begins.

The Bible contains stories of the judges, kings, prophets, apostles, defeats, victories, exile and return from exile. Also, the stories of Jesus, and the stories He told. We call them parables. The Bible is an extended story. Within the story framework there are songs, genealogies, letters, sermons, collections of wisdom, visions.

Whatever else Christianity is, it's based around a story, the story of Jesus' birth, life, death, resurrection and ascension.

131

Spirituality in a Mixed-Up Age

J.B. Phillips paraphrases the opening of Luke's account of Jesus' birth this way, "The story begins in the days when Herod was king of Judea ..." As Frederick Buechner points out, what the ancient, Christian creeds declare are really the events of a story, "a series of largely flesh and blood events that happened, are happening, will happen in time and space."①

Whatever else the Christian life is, it is a way of life based around this story of Jesus. Christian spirituality and story are thus closely connected.

A story is not just a statement of an idea, not just a doctrine or truth expressed in propositions. A story is a flesh and blood living out of some truth. It is truth translated into life, people, relationships.

Stories have great power. To make that point, let me tell you an old story.

Once upon a time, there was a sultan of Baghdad who had a nasty habit of executing women from his harem after spending the night with them. There was, however, one princess in his harem, Scheherezade, who was determined not to meet this fate. At the end of her "one night stand," she told the sultan a fascinating story. But, like a tantalizing soap serial episode, she stopped at a crucial point and wouldn't continue until the next night. The nasty sultan wanted to get on with the morning-after execution. However, he couldn't stand to kill Scheherezade and not know how the story ended. The princess lived to tell her story one more night. In fact, she lived to tell the sultan a story for 1,000 nights. Her stories kept her alive until she was too good to kill.

Stories have great power to grip us because they root reality in flesh and blood right where we live. I could ask you how you grew in your faith during the past year. You could give me a series of statements like, "I learned to trust God more"; "I

Stories and Spirituality

totally surrendered myself to Christ for the first time"; and "I became a better steward of my resources." On the other hand, you could tell me some real-life accounts of the living out of these growing edges in your life. Which would be the truest — the statements or the stories? Which would communicate best what happened in your life — the statements or the stories? Which would register most effectively with someone who is not a believer in Jesus — the statements or the stories?

Stories are also powerful because they express who we are. Stories teach and reveal identity. When families are together at holiday time, family stories are told. One Thanksgiving evening, when my small, extended family was together, I asked my parents to tell us about how it was "in the olden days." It was a little hard to get Mother and Dad going. But when they finally did get launched, we heard some wonderful stories, new to me, and some I'd heard several times before. During their childhood and teen-age years at their birthday celebrations, my two children were told again the stories of their births. This storytelling was a kind of birthday ritual. Stories help to foster or rekindle the sense of family unity and identity.

But why are stories and spirituality so closely linked? Salvation is communicated through story. The story in Scripture is an extended narrative of God's salvation. Christian spirituality is about where the story of salvation and the story of your life and mine intersect.

Frederick Buechner expresses concern if "the God you believe in as an idea doesn't start showing up in what happens to you in your own life." In other words, is He seen in your real, flesh and blood life's story? "If God is present anywhere, it is in those stories that God is present. If God is not present in those stories," writes Buechner, "then you might as well give up the whole business."[2]

133

Spirituality in a Mixed-Up Age

How much has the truth that we say we believe influenced our real-life, flesh and blood stories? Do I say I believe in a God of grace, but then live my story as if I served a God of constant and intense demand? Do I say I believe in prayer, but don't take time for prayer to be a significant part of my life's story? Do I say I believe in a God who has a special and tangible care for the poor, but live my life's story doing little or nothing to respond to people in poverty, here or across the world? What is in my real-life, flesh and blood stories is what I really believe, no matter how many belief statements I make. My story expresses what I experience of salvation. The story of Jesus and His salvation needs to intersect and become interwoven with my story.

One more observation about stories and spirituality: Christian spirituality is best expressed in stories. To put it another way, Christian witness is best conveyed in stories.

Usually, it's in a story that truth and reality are quietly, sometimes subtly communicated. When Jesus preached, He told stories. When Abraham Lincoln wanted to make a point, he told a story. In some cultures even today, when one asks a question, the answer may well be a story. Stories slip under our defenses and communicate powerfully to us. That's the strength of drama and film. They tell a story.

Furthermore, in Christian witness it's hard to argue with a story, especially if it's yours. The most powerful way to talk about God is to tell our own story of experiencing God and His Son, Jesus. True spirituality is seen when the truth of God's dealing with the human race becomes our story. Then we have something to share winsomely with others. Our stories are the most effective way to witness to those who do not know Jesus.

How does the church most effectively communicate the truth of the gospel in Christian worship? Through story.

Stories and Spirituality

Through a regular retelling, even reenactment of the story of Jesus' death in the Lord's Supper. Through an annual retelling of the Christian story, the story of Jesus.

Churches that follow the church year in worship have the opportunity, starting with Advent, Christmas and Epiphany, to Lent, Easter, Ascension and Pentecost to tell again and again the "old, old story" of Jesus. We do this through song and sermon, ritual and reenactment, art and the acts of worship. We use the musical and liturgical resources of our heritage and of today to tell the story of Jesus in language that contemporary people can understand.

A fully orbed Christian spirituality draws from each season of the church year. Every part of the Christian story contributes to a rich and balanced spirituality. For that reason, I want to highlight the message of the seasons and special days of the church year as they tell the Christian story.

The church year traditionally begins in Advent, the four weeks prior to Christmas Sunday and the celebration of Jesus' birth. But merging with that beginning of the Christian story are two other festivals that also help us make sense of spirituality. They are the commemoration of the Reformation at the end of October and Thanksgiving, close to a month later. It is appropriate, then, to begin our reflections on the seasons of the Christian story with the preludes of Reformation and Thanksgiving.

18
Roots and Renewal
— Transformation

On **October 31, 1517**, a spark ignited what we know as the Protestant Reformation. The source of that spark was Martin Luther, a 34-year-old German monk, professor of theology, preacher — not your classic revolutionary.

Luther and the Reformation were not about being anti-Catholic, but about being pro-Christian. Roman Catholics today affirm the contribution of Luther and use his great hymn "A Mighty Fortress" in worship services. Luther's hope was to reform the church not start a new one. His primary emphasis was on a reformed spirituality, a renewed understanding of how God works with human beings, and how we respond to God's initiatives.

Reformation spirituality involved a return to the roots of Christianity in the New Testament and early church. It attempted to go back before the distortions of medieval Christianity, back to the spring and source of the river instead of merely drinking at the wide, but muddy waters the river had become. A contemporary theologian writes, "Above all, the Reformation was a quest for Christian roots, grounded in the belief that a community that loses sight of its roots has lost sight of its reason for being in the world in the first place."[1] It was in such a return to the roots of faith that renewal and reform came about.

How important are roots anyway? A major element in

137

Spirituality in a Mixed-Up Age

the whole preoccupation with spirituality today is a quest for one's roots, a rediscovery of one's heritage. Why is St. Mark's Cathedral (Episcopal), located in secular Seattle, jammed for midnight services on Christmas Eve? Why are people interested in customs and ceremonies unique to their ethnic heritage? Why is St. Patrick's Day celebrated with greater fervor in New York City than in Dublin, Ireland? Why do Americans love Garrison Keillor's mythical small town of Lake Woebegone?

Even though most of us don't live in small towns, many of us came from small towns, and, even if we didn't, we idealize what small towns stand for → belonging, roots, a clear sense of who we are. In an age when people tend to be cut off from their biological roots, rediscovering who they are requires a rediscovery of their roots.

In the Bible, people were again and again reminded of their roots and urged to give attention to them. When the Hebrew people arrived in the land of promise, they were to bring an offering of the first fruits of the land to the Lord. Standing before God, they were to make a declaration of their roots, which began with the statement, "My father was a wandering Aramean" (Deuteronomy 26:5). It climaxed with the Exodus story and entry into the Promised Land. Why? Because it was in the declaration of their roots that they would know who they really were in this new land.

Why did Jesus institute what we call the Lord's Supper? "Do this in remembrance of me," Jesus said. The Lord's Supper takes us back to the roots of faith in the cross of Jesus. It is in those roots that we see who we are, a community of faith formed through the death and resurrection of Jesus, people who depend for salvation and spiritual life on the cross, people whose defining symbol is the cross of Jesus. Roots are central in defining who we are and how we should live.

Roots and Renewal — Transformation

What do we know about our roots? Americans can be so preoccupied with what's new that we lose sight of who we are and what we're all about. I fear that many contemporary American Christians are like cut flowers, brightly blooming for a while, but short-lived because of being severed from their roots. No, this is not an appeal for traditionalism. "We've never done it that way before" can be the seven last words of the church! The ways of the past can be a barrier to the relevance of the present.

But healthy tradition can be a motivating guide for effectively encountering today and tomorrow. Healthy tradition can help us change when we should. As someone has said, "Hindsight leads to foresight." What we have to fear is not tradition, which has been called "the living faith of the dead." What we have to fear is traditionalism, "the dead faith of the living."

There are at least three areas where we can learn about an authentic spirituality from the Reformation emphasis on the rediscovery of roots. For one thing, Reformation spirituality is rooted in Scripture.

Luther rediscovered the Bible as the basis from which truth could be mined, and the ground which nurtures growth in Christian spirituality. Attending a conference at which representatives of extremist groups were speaking, Luther listened to one of them relate his visions and supposed personal divine revelations. After his lengthy discourse, Luther uttered one sentence which destroyed the credibility of that speaker, "You have mentioned nothing of Scripture," he said.[2]

Luther not only believed in the authority of Scripture, but in its public and private reading. In his day, there was often only one Bible in the parish which was chained to a desk at the church. Because Luther believed the Scriptures should be accessible to the common person, he translated the Bible into German for his people.

Spirituality in a Mixed-Up Age

Reformed spirituality, whether in the 16th or 20th century, is rooted in Scripture. It involves reading the Bible as the basic resource for spiritual life. Authentic Christian spirituality is grounded in and nourished by the Scriptures.

Furthermore, Reformation spirituality is rooted in the character of God. We find out who we are by finding out who God is and what God is like.

Unfortunately, today, many people's ideas about spirituality have nothing to do with a clear understanding of God. People try to understand the inner life of human beings and the nonmaterial world of the spirit without beginning with a right view of God. Many moderns are big on angels, near-death experiences and special techniques for meditation. But they are not big on who God is and what God is like. That is where we must start!

The characteristic of God that had the greatest impact on Luther's life was grace. He spent his early adult years searching for a gracious God. In the monastery, he did all he could to satisfy what he thought were the demands of an angry God. But through preparing to lecture on Scripture, especially on Paul's epistles, Luther encountered a God of grace Who saved people not because of their effort or merit or good works, but solely because of His love. Reformed spirituality, whether in the 16th or 20th century, is rooted in a God who is holy and just but is also gracious and loving.

Finally, Reformed spirituality is rooted in life. One of the great achievements of the Reformation was to insist that the place of spirituality was not just the monastery but in the marketplace. Spirituality was not just for monks, but for mainline folk, who lived in the world, worked for a living, married and raised children and served God in the midst of the marketplaces of life.

Roots and Renewal — Transformation

The reformers believed in marriage and the home. At age 42, Luther himself married a former nun and lived out the gospel in the complexity of family life. Six children, as Luther liked to put it, were born "to a monk and a nun." Luther understood marriage and family life to be a "school for character," and it was in that very real life situation that spirituality was to be lived out.

Reformed spirituality gave work a new dignity. Christians have a calling to a work through which we are to live out our faith. Our work, whether paid or unpaid, is to be an act of praise and a way to honor God. Some have taken "the Protestant work ethic" to an extreme, becoming workaholics, loving their work too much. That is obviously not an asset to spirituality.

The reformers also believed not only in the priesthood of the ordained clergy, but in the priesthood of all believers. Every person had access to God directly and could help one another connect with God.

Reformation spirituality was rooted in life, everyday life. Authentic Christian spirituality must also be rooted in everyday life. What God's Spirit does in us must be lived out in homes, relationships, places of employment, our neighborhoods and in the world. For the God Who is revealed to us in Scripture, and the God in Whose character an authentic spirituality is rooted, is also the God Whose Son took our flesh and blood upon Him and lived our common life. Christian spirituality is to be an "earthy spirituality," lived out in the realities of everyday life.

Celebrating the Reformation every year calls us to reclaim our roots. It is through such a discovery and celebration of roots that we are constantly renewed in faith, kept fresh in spirit and guided in our encounters with the world as it is to-

Spirituality in a Mixed-Up Age

day. Ponder this thought: "The past is not dead; it holds the key to the future."³ Think about that and let the roots of the gospel and the heritage of the Christian faith be the means by which contemporary life and spirituality are nourished.

19

Taste and See — Thanksgiving

The **Thanksgiving season,** which merges into Advent, the traditional beginning of the church year, is a time of eating and often overeating. Maybe it's odd that in America we celebrate our thankfulness to God by eating up as much of His creation as possible in one sitting. But, before we feel too guilty, let's remember that eating is a wonderful biblical symbol of celebration, of enjoying the richness of God's provision. There is an ascetic spirituality that withdraws from the physical and material pleasures of life. That hardly squares with Scripture's vigorous celebration of all God's good gifts.

It's possible for Christian people to forget how to celebrate the goodness of life and of God, thinking of God as an oversized parent who loves to say no! By contrast, the poet-author of Psalm 34 urges, "Taste and see that the Lord is good!" (Psalms 34:8). Some scholars suggest that the word translated "see" could just as well be "and drink deeply" or "and drink your fill." This is a spirituality of thanksgiving, preoccupied not with negatives and prohibitions, but with the table laden with good things God provides.

One emphasis of the beautifully crafted Psalm 34 is this: Taste and see — even in trouble. The Lord is good even in the midst of difficulties. The psalm's heading describes a time when David was in trouble. The poem is full of references to adversity. The psalmist speaks of "the afflicted," of "this poor man

Spirituality in a Mixed-Up Age

who cried to the Lord," of people who are "brokenhearted and crushed in spirit." Twice he speaks of the Lord, "he delivers them from all their troubles" (verses 6 and 17).

At times, this good God delivers us out of trouble. At other times, this good God gives grace in the midst of trouble. In any event, and despite trouble, we are urged to "taste and see that the Lord is good." Trouble in life doesn't change God's goodness. And if we can't celebrate anything else, we can celebrate God for Who He is.

A TV news program brought the story of a grieving father who had just lost six children in a car accident. He did not hold the person driving the other vehicle to blame. "It was an accident," he said. As the cameras rolled, he said, "I thank God for the gift of six wonderful children." That's celebrating the goodness of God even in the midst of trouble.

The other, even more obvious theme of Psalm 34 is: Taste and see, with thanksgiving. "I will extol the LORD at all times; his praise will always be on my lips ... Glorify the LORD with me; let us exalt his name together" (verses 1 and 3).

Authentic Christian spirituality rejoices in the goodness of God and majors in giving thanks to Him. It is this celebration of God's goodness which gives life its sparkle and lift. Writes Henri Nouwen, "Without a spirit of gratitude, life flattens out and becomes dull and boring. But when we continue to be surprised by new manifestations of life and continue to praise and thank God and our neighbor, routine and boredom cannot take hold.

A 17th century Puritan paraphrase of Psalm 34 celebrates the consistent goodness of God:

"Through all the changing scenes of life,
In trouble and in joy,
The praises of my God shall still

Taste and See — Thanksgiving

My heart and tongue employ.
O magnify the Lord with me,
With me exalt His name.
When in distress to Him I called,
He to my rescue came."

Spirituality — Living Between the Already and the Not Yet

20

Advent: Promises and Hope

At a special dinner at our home, I asked for the rolls to be passed. Someone commented about too many rolls resulting in my added girth. I quickly defended myself by noting that bread is good for you, and that we had gone to some lengths to cut down on the fat in our diet, even resorting to using a bland butter substitute. As dinner conversations will, this one picked up on the product name. "*Promise*, wonder why it's called that." Someone quickly responded, "Why? Because it gives you hope for tomorrow!"

Advent, that period of four weeks before Christmas Sunday, is a time of promise, a time of hope. The spirituality that is nourished by this season of the church year is one of both hope and of waiting-hope because of the promise and waiting for its fulfillment. One of the themes of Advent is the Second Coming of Jesus, a promised event for which we hope and wait.

The scriptures themselves are full of promise and fulfillment as well as the living out of the period between the already and the not yet. Life is full of that waiting period between the pronouncement of the promise and its fulfillment. After my wife and I promised each other we would marry, we didn't do it until over a year later. When a child is born, there is the promise of a healthy member of the family and of society. But sometimes parents hold their breath and wait for that promise to be lived

Spirituality in a Mixed-Up Age

out in that human being's life. A waiting time is wrapped up in any promise. Someone has said, "Advent is the waiting season."

Waiting for medical test results can be foreboding. Waiting for a sermon to end may be tedious. But waiting can also be centered in eager anticipation, as in waiting for a loved one to exit a plane. Waiting is living between the already and the not yet, between the pronouncement of the promise and its fulfillment.

Between the visit of the angel to Mary and the Bethlehem stable were nine long months. Between the excited announcement, "We're going to have a baby!" and the wonder of delivery, there's being pregnant. Someone has suggested that what God has given women in the process of pregnancy, God has given the church in Advent. Pregnancy is a picture of Advent and a picture of authentic Christian spirituality. Living somewhere between the already and the not yet is where genuinely spiritual people reside.

One of the wonderful Advent stories is about a pregnant woman, Elizabeth. She and her husband Zechariah were wonderful senior adults, deeply devoted to one another, godly folk. However, there was sadness in their lives because they were unable to have children. In those days, since it was always thought to be the woman's fault, not producing a child was even considered by some as valid grounds for divorce, but Zechariah didn't divorce Elizabeth.

Now Zechariah was a priest; Elizabeth, the daughter of a priest. One day it fell to Zechariah's lot to offer incense on the temple altar. Because there were many priests, this might be a once in a lifetime opportunity. Zechariah went alone into the holy place and offered incense on the altar, while a crowd of people waited in prayer in the temple courtyard. When the people outside saw the smoke of incense rising from the altar,

Advent: Promises and Hope

they fell down before the Lord until the priest reappeared. But this time, there was an unusually long silence. People were getting edgy, like they do in prayer groups when there are long pauses between prayers. Some whisper to each other, "Wonder what's keeping him so long. Wonder if something has happened to him."

Finally Zechariah appeared in the courtyard. People's relief, however, turned to confusion because he couldn't say anything. Obviously agitated, he kept gesturing with his hands. "He's seen a vision!" was the courtyard-sweeping whisper. He had been visited by an angel who promised that Elizabeth would have a son to be named John.

Zechariah's initial alarm and surprise turned to disbelief. "Why, I'm an old man and my wife isn't young anymore! How can this be? How can I be sure this will happen?" Because of his unbelieving questioning, he had been struck with silence. When finished with his temple duties, Zechariah went home to Elizabeth and tried to communicate what had happened in the temple.

One challenge that comes to us from this beautiful story about promise is to believe the promise. When God is at work, we can believe His promises. "A promise from God," wrote 19th century English pastor, Charles Spurgeon, "may very instructively be compared to a check payable to order ... He is to take the promise," Spurgeon continued, "and endorse it with his own name by personally receiving it as true."

A second challenge from the story is to live out the promise.

Amazingly, the promise made to Zechariah began to be fulfilled. Elizabeth startled herself and her doctor by showing signs of pregnancy. Finally she said to her physician, "Let's just keep this thing under wraps until we know for sure it's really

151

Spirituality in a Mixed-Up Age

so. Please don't publish my case in the medical journals for at least five months." Elizabeth went into seclusion for those five months, choosing to be silent along with her husband. That silence involved waiting and living between the already and the not yet.

In nine months, the promise was fulfilled, and a baby was born. When the father indicates that his name is to be John, his tongue was loosed and his pent-up feelings burst forth in prophetic song. You can read it in Luke 1:67-69. The silence had been pregnant with promise, and out of that silence and the waiting came a great song of praise and prophecy.

Genuinely spiritual people live on the basis of promise while they wait for the promise to be fulfilled. Obviously, that doesn't mean we just sit back and do nothing. We also work toward the fulfilling of that promise.

Much troubled by her older brother's trapping of rabbits, a young girl resorted to prayer. Her mother overheard her, "Dear God, please stop Tommy from trapping rabbits. Please, don't let them get trapped. They can't. They won't! Amen." Perplexed, her mother asked, "Darling, how can you be so sure God won't let the rabbits be trapped?" The child calmly replied, "Because I jumped on the traps and sprung them!"

Christian spirituality involves believing the promise and working toward its fulfillment. It is believing God is at work in us through His Holy Spirit and then living on that basis.

A final challenge from the Zechariah and Elizabeth story was this, proclaim the promise. The baby, so unusual to these senior adults, became a great proclaimer of God's promises to His ancient people. John the Baptizer preached vigorously against sin, but he also proclaimed the promise of God, the coming of God's Messiah. A fulfillment of promise himself, John proclaimed the promise of God.

Advent: Promises and Hope

In an age when pessimism is rampant, when feelings of anger and alienation are commonplace, and when hope is superficial if there is any at all, Christians should be spreaders of hope. As we live on the basis of promise, we share our hope with those around us. Living hopefully, we proclaim God's promise between the already and the not yet.

But what happened to John? Didn't he get his head cut off? Yes, but he fulfilled the purpose for his life, which was to be the forerunner of the Messiah. John pointed people to Jesus, serving the kingdom of God, though it meant his life. Believing the promise, living the promise and proclaiming the promise doesn't mean life will be a "bed of roses" for us. It can be difficult living between the already and the not yet, but if we believe that the most important thing in life is to live for God and to be in relationship with Jesus Christ, we can live fully and hopefully. We can live this way in difficult times and even while we wait for the fulfillment of God's promises.

You may be discouraged because of the not yet, tired of waiting for the fulfillment of what you feel are God's promises. Take heart! The message of Advent is that God's promise is still true despite what seems like a long wait.

21
Why a Baby?

A famous preacher once said about the first Christmas, "God walked down the stairs of heaven with a baby in His arms."

That's nice! But why a baby? What good would a baby be? When the world needs saving and people need helping, when there's disrespect for authority, violence in schools, streets and homes, when drug use is on the rise among adolescents, and sexual misconduct is happening at all levels of society, what good is a baby?

Seven hundred years before the birth of Jesus, the prophet foretold the birth of a special baby. That infant would be born into a time of darkness and defeat for God's people but would be a sign of God's delivering presence among them. "To us a child is born," is Isaiah's prophetic word (Isaiah 9:6). This word applied to a historical child in the prophet's day but also foretold the coming of the Messiah who would deliver His people. But how do you connect deliverance and baby?

At Jesus' birth, the angel's announcement to sleepy shepherds outside Bethlehem contained two paradoxical words savior and baby. "Today, in the town of David a Savior has been born to you ... You will find a baby wrapped in cloths and lying in a manger" (Luke 2:11-12). Babies are weak and dependent. A baby is humanity in its most helpless stage. Yet, when God wanted to give a sign of His deliverance to the king of Is-

155

Spirituality in a Mixed-Up Age

rael in Isaiah's day, He pointed to a baby. Again, when God wanted to communicate Himself to us personally, unmistakably in Christ, He became a human baby.

C.S. Lewis in his inimitable manner expressed it this way, "The Eternal Being, who knows everything and who created the whole universe, became not only a man, but before that a baby, and before that a fetus inside a woman's body."[1]

We live in a culture preoccupied with power. That power is often linked with violence, the attempt by one person or group to exercise power over another person or group.

"The Mighty Morphin Power Rangers," once a popular children's show, generated $1 billion in retail sales, including $300 million in *Power Ranger* toys. Ninety-six percent of teachers polled witnessed Morphin-inspired acts of aggression at school.

In our power-preoccupied culture children are socialized early in the ways of power, usually understood to include violence. But God communicates Himself to us as a baby. Think of it, a weak, helpless, dependent baby!

Why a baby? To show us something about God and about how life works best. Christian spirituality is authentic only when it thinks and lives incarnationally, that is, on the basis of the baby.

An incarnational spirituality recognizes that God came to us in weakness, that is, as a baby.

In His entire life, this baby never achieved human power. His vocation was that of carpenter, a good, honest profession, but not one usually associated with power. In His teaching, He said, "If someone strikes you on the right cheek, turn to him the other also" (Matthew 5:39). At the end of His short ministry when people came unjustly to arrest Him, He could have defended Himself with the resources

Why a Baby?

of divine power but He did not. He gave Himself up to the weakness of death on a cross.

The birth of a weak, helpless baby is at the heart of the Christian message, and that's extraordinary! In fact, the whole Christmas story is extraordinary, not what people would have made up had they decided to start a new religion. This says profound things about the nature of authentic Christian spirituality. Ours is a spirituality symbolized by a baby.

With this basic truth as a foundation, think of some of its implications. For one thing, we come to God in receptivity. Not only did God become vulnerable in the Baby Jesus, but if we are to live in relationship with God, the only way is to be open, trusting, vulnerable to God.

When we are before God, we become like the baby — weak, dependent, receptive, unable to make it on our own. "Let the little children come to me," said Jesus, "... for the kingdom of heaven belongs to such as these" (Matthew 19:14). The only way to be a part of God's kingdom is to be as dependent and receptive as a baby.

Christian spirituality is not one of power but of weakness. It is openness to God and to His grace. It is humbly accepting God's gifts. It is trusting reliance upon God for salvation and for life. It is receptivity to God.

Another implication of the baby at the heart of Christian spirituality is this need. We relate to people out of vulnerability. God has modeled the way for us to communicate with each other. Since God approached us in the vulnerability of weakness, we are to approach one another not through the avenue of power but along the road of vulnerability.

Uniquely, Christian relationships involve being vulnerable to one another, open to one another, learning from one another, accepting one another, refusing to be manipulative,

Spirituality in a Mixed-Up Age

controlling and power-grabbing. The most effective communication is done not from a position of power but from one of loving vulnerability.

Marriages, family relationships, even church relationships often get into trouble because they are based on a power struggle. People vie for domination and control. People play the game of one-upmanship and can't communicate effectively because their highest priority is winning the power war in the relationship. Relationships work best and communication happens most effectively when it occurs out of the weakness of vulnerability.

A few years ago when I arrived on the campus of South India Biblical Seminary, where I was to teach for eight weeks, I had one of many periodic stomach upsets. "Delhi belly" was what we sometimes called the condition, not life-threatening but very uncomfortable. I was to speak in chapel the morning after we arrived. That day, I was pale and probably approached preaching somewhat less aggressively than usual. But I got through the message and sat down. Indian principal Narendra John whispered to me, "God often works best through our weakness."

The older I am, the less I am taken with loud, overconfident people who sound as if they're always on top of the world. The older I am, the more ready I am to admit that my own life isn't that way. I have a hard time identifying with Christian superstars, but I can identify with people weak like me through whom God nevertheless speaks and accomplishes His purposes.

A final observation from the weakness of the Baby Jesus is this: We look to the future with hope.

Christian spirituality starts not with power, but with a weak baby. That baby was like a time bomb, which would explode in the power structures of the world. In Isaiah's day the

Why a Baby?

baby was a sign that challenged even the greatest power in that age, the empire of Assyria. At the first Christmas, the baby was a sign which would challenge the greatest world power of that time, Rome.

These babies were like time bombs, ticking bundles of potentiality, threatening the power-hungry empires of the world. Weakness in the hands of God is ultimate power, gentle power, love-power, holy power. And in that time bomb of loving power there is hope that no matter how much the powers of this world seem in charge, God is still in control.

One day, it will be said, "The kingdom of the world has become the kingdom of our LORD and of His Christ, and he will reign for ever and ever" (Revelation 11:15). Baby-likeness can be a time bomb awaiting God's timing to challenge this world's power and bring God's kingdom fully into view.

I love the story of Roaring Camp, a California mining community that lived up to its name. Wild, rough, it was all men except one woman, Cherokee Sal. But she died while giving birth to a baby. The men decided they ought to care for the baby. They got an old box, stuffed rags in it and placed the baby in the box. Because one of the men decided that the rough box wasn't really suitable, he traveled 80 miles for a rosewood cradle. But then, the rags around the baby looked out of place.

Another man traveled to Sacramento for silk and lace blankets. Then, when the men bent over the lovely cradle, they noticed the floor. It was horribly dirty! Those hardened miners got down on hands and knees and scrubbed the floor clean. Of course, you know what that did to the walls and ceiling and windows. They too had to be washed and curtains hung.

The men found they had to give up fighting, for babies don't sleep well through a brawl. The miners liked to take the baby out to the mine, which they then decorated by planting

Spirituality in a Mixed-Up Age

flowers at the entrance. When some began to notice that against the soft skin of the baby their hands were dirty, the camp store sold out of soap, shaving lotion and perfume. The baby had changed everything!

Christmas calls us to a spirituality of incarnation. Christmas calls us to hope in the baby, not in the power structures of this world or in the symbols of status and power valued by our culture. Place your hope in the baby. It's this baby Who will facilitate change.

22

Promises Fulfilled

A full and annual retelling of Jesus' story in the faith community requires that we observe Epiphany. This festival was celebrated by the early church on January 6 with more intensity than the celebration of Christmas. Epiphany speaks of the manifestation of the Light of the World to the Gentiles, but Epiphany is also the story of seekers who did see.

The Magi, around whom Epiphany is centered, were seekers. Though not believers in the one true God of the Hebrews, at least at first, they were seekers. They sought truth through the signs of nature and the stars. And it was these seekers who were given the privilege of seeing. It was seekers who were led progressively to Bethlehem and finally came to worship the Christchild.

There are many kinds of seekers then and now. A man regularly attended our church before moving to another city. He was raised in Roman Catholicism but became soured on institutional Christianity. He had very little contact with the church and the gospel message through his young adult years and early professional life. But in the aftermath of some painful life experiences, his heart was opened to God. He began to seek God. He made a faith commitment on his own, after which he showed up at the Free Methodist church near his home seeking to figure out what it was that he had done. For several months

Spirituality in a Mixed-Up Age

this young attorney was a regular attender at worship. He was a seeker who had found God, but continued to seek for what that meant in his life.

Another seeker, hypothetical but real, wants to be a Christian, but she is working through several issues. Some are doctrinal and lifestyle issues. She struggles with patterns of behavior which she would like to change. She's a seeker, but some longtime Christians are impatient with her. They want her to clean up her act, straighten up her life and quit asking so many questions. They want this all overnight. Some Christians are impatient with the process, the sometimes slow process of seeking and seeking and gradually finding.

Then, there's the man raised in the church, but who had wandered away from God and faith. Life has been hard on him. His own resources have proved woefully inadequate. He has realized his need for strength outside himself to cope with his difficulty. He is trying to find his way back to the faith of his family and of his childhood. He is a seeker after the faith he once knew.

Another seeker, this time a Christian, has been in the church for years. She is, however, always pushing the boundaries and exploring the frontiers. She raises troubling questions, not because she wants to be difficult, but because they genuinely concern her. She's a seeker → a believer and a seeker → one who believes there's always more to learn and always something fresh to experience of God.

"Shadowlands" is a Hollywood portrayal of the relationship between Oxford scholar and Christian writer, C.S. Lewis, and American, Joy Davidman Gresham. C.S. Lewis marries Joy late in life. Joy develops cancer; it goes into remission, but she dies after only a few short years of marriage. The grief of this man, who'd been a bachelor most of his adult life, is immense,

162

Promises Fulfilled

and none of the platitudes offered by Christian and academic friends help. In the midst of his grief, Lewis seeks an understanding of God that will encompass the tragedy he's experienced. He is a man seeking for meaning in the midst of pain and loss.

Contemporary society is filled with seekers. Secularism does not and cannot satisfy. Materialism comes up empty-handed. Seeking pleasure merely for itself is a dead-end street.

People these days are seeking for something spiritual. But are they finding it? Are they finding what the Magi of old found? Often not! Their quest is often for something merely inside themselves and not centered in the person of Jesus. And for many, the quest results in one more disillusioning failure to find reality and meaning.

Epiphany most readily happens to those who seek, but not all seeking results in seeing. If it is to be effective, seeking after the light must include some of the characteristics of the Magi's search so many centuries ago.

The seeking of the Magi included forsaking the comfort of security. They didn't just hop a plane to Jerusalem and catch an air-conditioned bus to nearby Bethlehem. There was no freeway system connecting with the Bethlehem road. In fact, they didn't know they were going to Bethlehem! Embarking on a journey into the unknown, they left behind what they knew. Often that's scary! It's threatening to push beyond the status quo and to ask questions you've never asked before and for which there may be no simple answers.

Sometimes, young adults come to college, even to Christian schools, where they are asked to question some things they've always assumed. That can be uncomfortable for them and their parents. At times, adults in middle years begin to question the basic assumptions on which their lives and careers

163

Spirituality in a Mixed-Up Age

have been built, wondering if they have to live the balance of their years the same way.

Occasionally, people that are settled in predictable patterns of life, in comfortable careers, feel called to launch out into something new and different, to change careers, to enter an occupation more conducive to living out their faith, maybe even to go into some form of Christian ministry. These experiences can be uncomfortable. But seeking involves forsaking the comfort of security.

2. A second dimension to the Magi's seeking was following the light to Christ. That following required persistent obedience. Their's was not a quick and easy quest. We think of the Magi arriving at the manger just after the shepherds, who hiked in from the nearby hills. But manger scenes and Christmas pageants notwithstanding, the Magi weren't at the manger. Matthew's reference to the Christchild speaks of a toddler, not an infant. It may have been months, up to two years after Jesus' birth that the Magi finally arrived. Their journey was a long one and required obediently following the light day after day. It was, as Eugene Peterson describes the Christian journey, "a long obedience in the same direction."

Furthermore, their obedient following was in a definite direction. The Magi were not aimlessly wandering here and there, following this and that ray of light. There was a definite star which led to Jesus. In healthy seeking today, Jesus Christ is the object and goal of the search. This is where so many contemporary spiritual quests miss. People look to mystical experiences of one kind or another. People follow this teacher or that cult. They go to seminars, spiritual retreats, 12-step groups, and various kinds of therapy, all of which may have value but may or may not be focused on Jesus. Jesus is the light that serious seekers must follow. And it is to Him that we journey.

Promises Fulfilled

Finally, seeking in the manner of the Magi involves finding the Christ in worship. Matthew tells us they "bowed down and worshiped Him." Their quest was satisfied not just in orthodox doctrine or correct words about Jesus. If it had been, then once they had found the right words, their quest would have ended.

The object of the Magi's seeking was not just words but worship. And worship involves relationship. There is no end to the ways a relationship can grow and develop. Worship can grow richer as one continues to seek and continues to see.

Listen to Paul's word to the Philippian Christians, a word that expressed his lifelong seeking and seeing: "Not that I have already attained or am already perfected; but I press on, that I may lay hold of that for which Christ Jesus has also laid hold of me. one thing I *do*, forgetting those things which are behind and reaching forward to those things which are ahead, I press toward the goal for the prize of the upward call of God in Christ Jesus" (Philippians 3:13-14, NKJV).

Let's never quit being seekers! It's a good thing to be a seeker! And let's not be impatient with seekers in the church! Authentic Christian spirituality is a seeking spirituality, always open to new and fresh light in relationship with Christ, accepting and understanding of other people's quests after truth and reality.

Spirituality — From the Depths to the Heights

23

The Cross: A Sob and a Song

Some time ago, a Peter Jennings news program, entitled "In the Name of God," surveyed ways some churches are trying to reach contemporary society. It was a remarkably fair presentation without the negative slant sometimes presented in the media. One point came across to me as I watched this program. It was the apparent effort by the churches to portray Christianity as always positive, upbeat, happy.

One group was led into "holy laughter." The statement was made that people came to the service depressed and left happy. Now, I'm not against laughing in church. I'm all for joyful, celebrative worship. But if we are to be true to Scripture and true to the realities of life, we need to acknowledge and deal with the darker side of life in worship as well.

This is an important theme for the Lenten season, a six-week period leading up to Holy Week, a season characterized by a cross-focus. The spirituality of this season of the church year helps us come to grips with the darker side of life. Even Christians who celebrate the resurrection of Jesus, who live in the joy of the Lord, and who experience peace and hope, nevertheless need to deal with this darker side of life.

This is certainly something Jesus experienced also. Jesus wept at a friend's grave, angry at death's power. Jesus experienced the agony of being forsaken and betrayed by friends

Spirituality in a Mixed-Up Age

and followers. Jesus went through a tremendous conflict of spirit in the Garden of Gethsemane where He cried out to be freed from having to go through what was ahead of Him. Jesus went through the awful physical pain and suffering of flogging and being nailed to a cross. On the cross Jesus felt separated even from God, His Father. He cried out in agony, "My God, why have you forsaken me?" Jesus experienced the darker side of life, too. Jesus went through that darkness for you and me. Jesus goes through that darkness with you and me.

Early Christians understood that the cross was not a happy symbol. In fact, very early Christians tried hard to find other symbols for their faith, the fish, rainbow, dove — anything but the cross. The cross was the cruelest form of capital punishment ever invented by human beings. It was an instrument of torture. Many in the Roman Empire had seen people publicly crucified. The cross was not a happy symbol.

Protestants often wear and display crosses. We wear them around our necks and have them in places of worship. But it's usually a plain, empty cross because we want to emphasize the resurrection, the reality of Easter. If you visit a Roman Catholic Church, however, you will see a crucifix, a cross with the figure of Jesus still on it. Some Christians in the church I serve have told me that they wear a crucifix because they don't want to forget His sufferings.

It is possible for Protestants to be so Easter oriented in our spirituality that we do not walk with Jesus through His sufferings. And when we do not have a spirituality of the cross, life can be shallow, superficial, insufficiently tuned to the reality of suffering. When we do not have a spirituality of the cross, we may be ill-prepared to meet suffering when it comes to us.

There are dark days with veils and shadows. There are struggles, uncertainties, questions, discouragement, anger.

The Cross: A Sob and a Song

There is pain, illness, death. And these dark and difficult experiences are also a part of real life even for good people and godly people. You may even be there today.

The psalms are filled with praise and joy. They exult in God, offering thanksgiving to Him. But the psalms aren't all happy songs. In fact, they run the full gamut of human emotion from exaltation to despair, from praise to anger, from adoration to complaint. Lament is the term used to describe some of the darker songs. In fact, the largest single category of psalms includes the psalms of lament → more in number than the psalms of thanksgiving.

When I was young, I used to be rather troubled at all the unhappy and angry stuff in the psalms. Does this bother you? But the more I experience of life, the more relieved I am that this is addressed in the Bible. For it's not just the happiness which connects with my life and yours. It's also the unhappiness and angry things which realistically connect with the way our life is.

Jesus was probably reciting one of these psalms of lament on the cross. Good Jew as He was, He knew many of the psalms by heart. Psalm 22 expressed what Jesus was going through with remarkable clarity. In fact, some suggest that David, the poet, must also have been a seer into the future. Maybe David didn't know that was what he was doing, but his poem seems to look beyond his own experience to that of the coming Messiah.

Someone has observed 13 reasonable parallels between Psalm 22 and the story of the cross. "A Sob and a Song" is one title for Psalm 22.

Feel the sob first. You feel the sob in the first 21 verses of the poem. Listen again and sense the poet's darkness. "My God, my God, why have you forsaken me? Why are

171

Spirituality in a Mixed-Up Age

you so far from saving me, so far from the words of my groaning?" (verse 1). This opening lament is parallel to the 10th psalm, which cries out, "Why, O Lord, do you stand far off? Why do you hide yourself in times of trouble?" I showed that verse recently to a person with no background in faith who had recently made a commitment to Christ but had experienced a major loss in his life. He looked at the words and said, "Do you mean that's in the Bible?" It is!

Psalm 22's lament contains the feeling that though the poet calls out to God in prayer, there is no response. There is the sense of being insignificant, worse yet, the feeling of being despised in the eyes of others. Physical symptoms often accompany dark feelings. Some feelings come when people seem out to get you, when enemies threaten you. These are the feelings of a sob. And these are part of most, if not every person's life experience.

What's your experience of the sob? Some Christians are sunny folks, sanguine, happy by temperament, not experiencing the darker side of life very intensely. That's OK. Some people's life experiences have been primarily positive, with very little of the trouble that dogs other people's footsteps. The challenge for sunny and optimistic people is to understand and empathize with the darkness others feel. Their challenge will be to accept and live through the darker experiences of life when they do come rather than being blown away by them.

Some Christians are more melancholic by temperament. They know by experience what it's like to be depressed. You may have gone through more than your share of difficult circumstances. And you really understand what the sob experience is all about.

The sob in some people's lives comes from carrying the baggage of the past. For some, the sob is about what's going on

The Cross: A Sob and a Song

right now. You've lost a love or lost a loved one. You feel rejected, betrayed, angry. You've failed at something and you feel ashamed. You've done something you know is wrong and you feel guilty. You're confused about life. You aren't sure quite what to believe anymore. And a sob is what you feel.

Everybody must walk through some dark valleys. That's the way life is, even for good people. And that's the way it was for Jesus. In addition to what He accomplished on the cross for our salvation, Jesus experienced the most intense kind of human darkness on the cross.

Jesus went through one huge sob on the cross and in the hours preceding it. One of the seven spoken words from the cross was the agonized cry already mentioned. Jesus, probably quoting from Psalms 22:1, cried out, "My God, why have you forsaken me?" This has been called the most staggering sentence in the gospel record. I used to think this meant that for a while God turned away from Jesus on the cross. Jesus was carrying the sins of the world and a holy God cannot look on sin. That may be true. But just as true is the understanding that on the cross Jesus experienced the darkest, the most God-forsaken sense of aloneness which humans can feel. "My God, why have you forsaken me?" One huge sob. In that cry, Jesus identified with the most intense human sob.

A realistic spirituality leaves room for the sob. It isn't merely preoccupied with happy endings, wonderful victories and neat solutions. A spirituality of the cross reminds us during the Lenten season of this darker side of life and helps us experience it in the context of our faith.

But in Psalm 22, we see reflected not only a sob but also a song. As is often the case in the psalms of lament, the sob, the complaint, the anger, the expression of sorrow and suffering isn't the last word. I'm glad of that! David often moved

173

Spirituality in a Mixed-Up Age

quickly from complaining bitterly about his enemies to praising the Lord for His great goodness.

For example, in Psalms 55:15, the poet screams to God, "Let death take my enemies by surprise; let them go down alive to the grave, for evil finds lodging among them." Truly angry words! But in the very next verse, the tone changes dramatically, "But I call to God, and the Lord saves me." Later in Psalms 55:22, "Cast your cares on the Lord and he will sustain you ..." Sob and song don't seem far apart.

In the first 21 verses of Psalm 22, there is an alternation between complaint and affirmation. After verse 22, the poet's heart and voice are more consistently lifted in song. He sees himself at a thanksgiving meal. He has brought a thank offering as prescribed by the law. That offering of an animal was to be eaten on the same day. And those who joined in the meal would join him in the offering of thanks and praise to God.

On such an occasion, "The poor will eat and be satisfied; those who seek the Lord will praise him — may your hearts live forever" (Psalms 22:26).

David also sees the praises of God extending beyond the boundaries of Israel. "All the ends of the earth will remember and turn to the Lord ..." (verse 27). Even future generations will proclaim the righteousness of the Lord.

This is the song which intersects and follows the experience of the sob. True to human life, there is a sob. But also, true to God's grace there can be a song right next to a sob and even in the midst of a sob. The poet, William Blake, wrote:

"Joy and woe are woven fine,
A clothing for the soul divine,
Under every grief and pine
Runs a joy with silken twine.
It is right it should be so;

The Cross: A Sob and a Song

Man was made for joy and woe;
And when this we rightly know
Through the world we safely go."

Back once more to Jesus on the cross. "My God, why have you forsaken me" is the cry wrung from a heart feeling the aloneness which most humans experience at one time or another. But, after this, just before He died, Jesus was also heard to say, "Father, into your hands I commit my spirit" (Luke 23:46). There was once more the fatherly sense of God's presence. It wasn't just "My God," but now "Father ..." It was as if His sob had developed into a song of trust. If Jesus was reciting Psalm 22 on the cross, the progression of that psalm led him from sob to song.

An early Christian leader, Clement of Alexandria, said, "Christ turns all our sunsets into dawns." The night may seem interminable. The sob may seem to last and last, and we have to accept and allow for this darker side of life. But the morning will come. "Weeping," sings Psalms 30:5, "may remain for a night, but rejoicing comes in the morning."

Anglican pastor and hymnwriter Henry Francis Lyte lay dying. Several weeks earlier his health broke, and he wrote his last and best-loved hymn. A few days before he died he put the finishing touches on it. Listen to the final stanza, written by a man whose sob of death had been turned into song:

"Hold thou thy cross before my closing eyes:
Shine thru the gloom and point me to the skies;
Heaven's morning breaks, and earth's vain shadows flee:
In life, in death, O Lord, abide with me."
His sob had become a song.

The spirituality of the cross deals realistically with suffering and darkness but chooses to praise God in the midst of it all. Can we do that? Will we do that?

175

Spirituality in a Mixed-Up Age

One Friday evening Bob Hanington, one of our church members, died. He had told me that at the age of 25, he was on skid row, an alcoholic as he put it, "worth nothing to anybody." But Bob encountered the gospel and responded in faith. He turned from his alcohol and became a Christian for the remainder of his 89 years. Out of the sob of his early life came the song of faith.

Over the last few months Bob had to be in a nursing home. Because he was alert and sharp in mind, while many around him were not, this was very hard for him. This was for Bob another dark time in his life. There was no getting around the lamentable experiences in the nursing home. Bob didn't so much complain to me as lament what he had to go through. How did he cope? He told me he prayed and slept a lot. Bob experienced a song in the midst of his sob.

24

Easter: A Time to Laugh

There's a great Old Testament story that's not usually associated with Easter. It's a story about life and laughter, and that's what Easter spirituality is about.

Here's Sarah, who lived 2,000 years before Jesus. She eavesdropped on her husband Abraham's conversation with messengers from God. They told Abraham that God would fulfill His promise to provide him a son. Sarah, 90 years old, was amused at this thought! She laughed to herself at the news that from her womb would come life. "Why did Sarah laugh?" asked the messengers of God (Genesis 18).

Nine months later, when this senior adult bore a child, she said, "God has brought me laughter and everyone who hears about this will laugh with me" (Genesis 21:6). She named her son Isaac, which means laughter.

Centuries after Sarah, the Hebrew poet sang about the time when his people came back from captivity in Babylon. "Our mouths were filled with laughter, our tongues with songs of joy" (Psalms 126:2).

Centuries later, the Apostle Paul wrote to Christians in the Greek city of Corinth about how they ought to give offerings to the Lord. They were probably not wealthy people; few of the early believers were. But Paul told them their giving ought to be done cheerfully. He used the word from which we get hilarious (2 Corinthians 9:7). Christians ought to be hilarious giv-

Spirituality in a Mixed-Up Age

ers. Christians ought to give their offerings with laughter.

Did you know that in the Eastern Orthodox Church there is a tradition of holy laughter at Easter? It's not the ecstatic laughter of some Christians today. It's more a liturgical laughter but nonetheless laughter. It's the laughter of faith. The explanation in the Eastern Orthodox Church is that worshipers laugh at the trick God played on the devil by raising Jesus from the dead.

This Easter laughter is the invasion of life into death, of light into darkness, of joy into sadness. Easter laughter is the gift of life in Sarah's womb. It is the liberation of God's people from bondage. It is the celebration of giving in the midst of poverty. It is also the messengers at the empty tomb who announce, "He is not here. He is risen!"

Why do people laugh? Some laugh out of cynicism or skepticism. Theirs is the laugh of unbelief. When the first people to the tomb on Easter morning reported what they had found, the other disciples laughed at them. After all, they were only credulous women! Who could believe their report? That's what they thought.

In Athens, when the Apostle Paul preached to philosophers about Jesus, they gave him respectful attention. When he got to the resurrection of the dead, however, the response was different. Some laughed that this preacher should believe such a thing (Acts 17:32, J.B. Phillips).

We also laugh when we think something is funny. There's health-giving, even life-giving laughter in humor. Norman Cousins, who fought off a serious disease with two hours a day of Marx Brothers films and "Candid Camera" reruns, talked about laughter as "internal jogging." Sarah did that kind of jogging. She was tickled at the amusing idea of her bearing a child, amused at God's wonderful surprise.

178

Easter: A Time to Laugh

> Some people laugh when they hear good news in the midst of darkness. Sarah's laugh, though very amused and even a little skeptical, was also the expression of a woman who had longed for children but had not been able to conceive. There had been great darkness in her life because of her inability to have a child. Now, she heard news that she would conceive and give birth to a child. Unbelievable! Amazing! Wonderful! Great, good news in the midst of her sadness of spirit. She laughed when God broke into her barrenness to bring life. This is uniquely Easter laughter.

My wife and I were in Indiana preparing to go to a funeral home. Her father had died unexpectedly only 10 months after her mother. I had interrupted a study leave in Vancouver, rushed back to Seattle, and we flew to Indiana. We were getting ready to go to the funeral home to view her father's body and then to engage in hours of greeting people who would come to pay their respects.

The funeral would be the next day. After that we faced the task of breaking up a household. Sobering task! Big job! It wasn't exactly a happy day.

But just as we were to leave the house, the phone rang. Our daughter Joy, from California, had some wonderful, good news. She had passed her nursing boards! She had been a little unsure of herself on the day of testing, and a lot was riding on the results. And as I heard this good news over the phone, I remember laughing – laughing wildly – half laughing and half crying. It was wonderful to have that gift of good news in the midst of a hard situation. That's Easter laughter.

Two heartsick people were on their way home on the afternoon of the first Easter Sunday. Terribly sad, their steps were slow, weighed down by dismay, disappointment, disillusionment, distress at circumstances they didn't understand. They

Spirituality in a Mixed-Up Age

were rehashing what had happened during the past week in Jerusalem, culminating in that awful scene on the hill outside the city. The One on whom they had pinned their hopes had been crucified between two criminals. They had, of course, celebrated Sabbath in the city, spending a sorrowful day with the other disciples. Then, just before they were to set out for their home in Emmaus, a few miles away, there had been all that commotion about Jesus not being in the tomb where He'd been placed on Friday. Nobody could figure out where His body was.

"Let's go home," they had said to one another.

That's how they happened to be trudging back to Emmaus on that first Easter day. But, in their darkness of spirit, they came upon a fellow traveler headed their way. He had overheard their discussion of the events of the past week and asked what it was all about. "Do you mean to tell us you don't know what has been going on in Jerusalem the last few days?"

"Tell me about it," He said.

One more time they related their sad story to Him. But when they finished, this stranger on the road began to talk, explaining to them from the law and the prophets the reason for Jesus' suffering and death. Since there were no motels in Emmaus, they invited Him to stay for dinner and for the night. At dinner, He, the guest, took charge and became the host. He broke bread, offered the thanksgiving prayer for the meal and began to pass food to them. Suddenly they recognized Him. But just as suddenly, He vanished.

What do you think they did when they knew it had been Jesus? Did they laugh? I'm sure they did! Half laughing, half crying for joy, they hurried quickly back to Jerusalem to tell their story. Did the other believers laugh when they heard this joyful good news? I think they did! I think there were some big belly laughs by Galilean fishermen that day!

Easter: A Time to Laugh

That's what Easter laughter is. It's a ray of light shining into darkness. It's the intrusion of joy into the heaviness of death. It's hope where there had been discouragement, even despair.

Every Easter we go through Good Friday first. All of us go through our Good Fridays. In fact, a lot of life is lived at the level of Good Friday. Good Friday is the place of darkness, suffering, difficulty, sorrow, discouragement. It's the place of the sob. And, as we've already observed, we need to accept and live through that sob. That's life!

But Good Friday is also the place of incompleteness. The cross is incomplete without the resurrection. Martin Luther suggested that we think of human existence as being like that first Good Friday. We see things that puzzle us and frighten us and don't feel complete. Our reason may lead us to conclude God is somehow unable or unwilling to be active in human affairs. Reason tells us there is little hope in the midst of life. Despair is thus a valid and reasonable response.

That's just the way life can be. Good Friday doesn't feel like Easter yet. Despite all the excitement of Easter morning, it still feels like Good Friday to some people. They've been through difficult days. They know suffering is supposed to be good for them but have had all the good they think they can tolerate for now. Though they know Easter Sunday is true, it may still feel like Good Friday. Easter laughter is the breaking in of resurrection reality upon our Good Friday darkness. Easter laughter is an awareness of completeness, fulfillment in the resurrection of Jesus. Easter laughter is the dawning of hope.

Christians are people who laugh like it's Easter, even when it may feel and look like Good Friday. That's what Easter spirituality is all about. Some people may say, "Oh, that's just whistling in the dark." No, that's laughing in the dark and that's OK!

Spirituality in a Mixed-Up Age

Christians are people who look at the Good Friday character of much of human life from the perspective of Easter. Sometimes that look and that laughter of Easter is by faith, not by feeling. By faith, we see all of the incompleteness, suffering and sadness of this life and this world in the light of Easter morning. By faith, we see that God is strangely, mysteriously at work, even when it feels like He is silent or inactive. By faith, and because of Easter, what seemed dark when viewed from the standpoint merely of human reason now looks full of hope. Easter breaks in upon what is merely reasonable and gives us God's viewpoint on the situation.

Someone has put it this way, "What looks like divine absence is really hidden divine presence." Christians laugh during Easter because this day brings new light to all our reasonable despair.

When the famous agnostic, Robert Ingersoll, died the funeral program had this solemn instruction, "There will be no singing." Why? There was no Easter faith. There was no Easter laughter in the face of death.

Christian spirituality faces the darkness of life and death, the sobs, the "Good Fridayness" of existence but lets the laughter of Easter filter through the cracks into that darkness. That laughter rejoices that Jesus is alive and present today. That laughter says death need not be the end of everything but rather the beginning of a new kind of life.

A journalist told of listening to a Russian lecturer in Moscow in the days before the Communist regime crumbled. He attacked the Christian faith for 90 minutes, proving to his satisfaction, at least, that faith in God was a dying survivor of capitalism. When he invited discussion, a village priest asked permission to speak.

"Not more than five minutes," responded the lecturer.

182

Easter: A Time to Laugh

"I shall not be long," replied the priest.

He ascended the platform and addressed the audience. "Brothers and sisters, Christ is risen!"

As one, the people responded with the familiar Russian, Easter greeting, "He is risen indeed!"

"I have finished," said the priest. "I have nothing more to say."

The laughter of Easter spirituality had intruded on the darkness of unbelief.

25

Pentecost: From Bones to Body

Six weeks after Easter, the annual telling of the Christian story comes to Ascension Sunday, and then, the following week, to Pentecost. These two great Sundays highlight the person and work of the Holy Spirit, both in the individual and in the community of believers, the church.

Elsewhere, we have thought together about the Holy Spirit and spirituality, as evidenced in one of the pinnacle chapters of the Bible, Romans 8. Descriptions of a Pentecost spirituality, however, are found not just in the book of Acts or the Pauline Epistles. The Holy Spirit is the Spirit of God from the beginning, as indicated in great pre-Pentecost Day, Old Testament spirit passages.

Central to Pentecost spirituality, whether illustrated by the Old or New Testaments, is the concept of life. The Holy Spirit is the bearer of a particular kind of life without which spirituality is reduced merely to the best our human insight and effort can produce. Pentecost spirituality is about life which restores to wholeness and unites in community.

Nowhere in Scripture is there a more dramatic portrayal of this life of the Spirit than in Ezekiel 37 and the Hollywood-worthy picture of a valley of dry bones, which, through the impact of the Spirit, became a dynamic body. Nowhere in Scripture is there a more relevant portrayal of the life-giving

Spirituality in a Mixed-Up Age

Spirit poured into profoundly needy human vessels than here in the prophecy of Ezekiel.

The need of exiled Hebrews in Babylon, for whom Ezekiel was pastor, is clear. No church today needs life more than did the disspirited, discouraged, disheartened, defeated captives in Babylon. They were people who felt like dry bones, a whole valley of dry bones. Ezekiel's vision aptly pictured their corporate self-image.

"Can these bones live?" was the question. The answer seemed clear. Bones long dead and dried up, bones disconnected from one another simply do not come to life. Or do they? But something amazing happened in pastor Ezekiel's picture. The bones come together with a rattling noise. They become encased in flesh, muscle, sinew and skin. They come to life and become bodies with breath flowing through them. These now-resurrected bones stand on their feet like a great army ready for action.

How did this come about? Through the power of God's Spirit communicated through the preaching of truth. That's what made the impossible happen. I know some preaching puts folks to sleep. Here's preaching which brought dead folks to life!

The bottom line to this picture → "I will put my Spirit in you and you will live ..." (verse 14). What made the difference was Spirit. The word Ezekiel used could mean breath, desert wind, powerful, energizing, unpredictable. But it's a word which also speaks of the Spirit of God Who is like breath and like desert wind. It's the Spirit Who gives life to dead bones. It's the Spirit Who brings restoration to people in captivity, whose image of themselves is like a valley of dry bones. It's the Spirit Who connects bone to bone in a dynamic, living body, making community possible. It's the Spirit Who brings about a living spirituality in both individual and church.

Pentecost: From Bones to Body

Centuries after Ezekiel, two men stood on a Jerusalem housetop one evening, talking about the fundamentals of the spiritual life. The older of the two was a respected rabbi and leader of the Jewish people. The other was a young rabbi, whose preaching had burned into the hearts of those who listened to Him. As they still do in Asia, these two were on a flat rooftop trying to catch whatever whiff of breeze there might be.

"The wind blows wherever it pleases. You hear its sound, but cannot tell where it comes from or where it is going ..." (John 3:8), said the younger of the two as they drew their cloaks about them because of the cool night air. As the evening breeze rustled their garments, Jesus said to Nicodemus, "I tell you the truth, no one can enter the kingdom of God unless he is born of water and the Spirit" (John 3:5).

Again, it's the Spirit Who brings the life of God into human beings, the Spirit Who makes possible restoration to friendship with God and thus to wholeness, the Spirit Who incorporates newly enlivened people into a community of living beings. It's the Spirit who turns dry bones into a dynamic body.

Something significant happened a couple years after this evening conversation, after the young rabbi had been crucified on a cross, after the older rabbi had finally come out of the closet as one of Jesus' supporters, after Jesus' miraculous restoration to life. His followers were gathered in prayer, celebrating the Jewish festival of Pentecost when an amazing thing happened. These followers of a crucified but now resurrected Jesus were all filled with the breath of God, the same breath about which Jesus spoke to Nicodemus, the same breath which brought life to the army of dead, disconnected bones in Ezekiel's vision. Again, with these Christians, that Spirit brought life, restoration and community.

But what about today? Life, restoration, community —

Spirituality in a Mixed-Up Age

that's what the Spirit of God is about both for individuals and for groups of believers. Even today, God wants to make dead bones into a dynamic body.

A Pentecost spirituality keeps ever open to the breath of God, giving the Spirit access to individual lives and to churches. A Pentecost spirituality is about life in all its varied forms, about restoration to the vitality and wholeness that God desires for us, and to a sense of community which God wants to be the vehicle for the Spirit in the world. The church I serve celebrates Pentecost with red and white balloons, breath-filled balloons that festoon the sanctuary on this Sunday. At the close of each service, worshipers take a balloon and we together release them, symbolizing the release of the Spirit into the world through His people.

Spirituality and Stewardship

26

Creation Stewardship

According to Ben Patterson, "Asking church members to give money is not fundamentally different from making an altar call or encouraging a parishioner to read the Bible."[1] How closely is Christian stewardship linked with Christian spirituality?

On Pentecost Sunday, as the congregation filed into church, ushers handed each person a red carnation to symbolize the festive spirit of the day. People heard the Pentecost story from the book of Acts. The sermon began, "The Spirit of the Lord is upon us. ..." A woman in the front pew shouted back, "Like the powerful wind from heaven!" And she threw a red carnation toward the altar. The preacher began again, "The spirit of the Lord is upon us!" The same woman's voice rang out, "Like tongues of fires. ..." She threw another carnation toward the altar. The preacher looked straight at her and said, "Now, sister, throw your pocketbook." To this the woman replied softly, "Preacher, you have just calmed the wind and put out the fire."

How are stewardship and spirituality connected?

The Bible teaches that one is incomplete without the other. Spirituality without stewardship is barren, unfruitful and empty, a little like the Apostle James' "faith without works," which is dead. On the other hand, a stewardship emphasis without a strong concern for a developing spirituality is naked, stark

191

Spirituality in a Mixed-Up Age

and subject to all sorts of distortions. A healthy and biblical stewardship grows out of the fertile soil of Christian spirituality.

There are at least two big, biblical themes which tie stewardship and spirituality together. These are foundational themes in the Bible → major ideas. By the way, I believe in the motivating power of big thoughts. I dislike urging people to put money in the offering merely because the church needs to pay its bills. Christians need to be committed to a grand and biblical world view, involved in big-picture spirituality, out of which our stewardship practices will grow and become fruitful.

If Christians give money simply because of a felt obligation to an organization, then we've missed a big part of Christian stewardship. If giving is just to provide us something we want, like Christian education, good church music, warm fellowship and impressive, functional buildings, then we have missed a large part of the Christian stewardship.

On a cold Sunday in January this note appeared in the bulletin of an upstate New York church: "Churches were not heated in the Middle Ages. Add $1 a week to your contribution to keep this custom from being renewed."

In contrast, Christian stewardship must grow out of a spirituality which responds gladly and obediently to what God has done for us. Here is where we come to these big, biblical ideas, which I am convinced tie stewardship and spirituality together. One of these themes is Creation, the other Exodus. There is a Creation spirituality, and there is an Exodus spirituality. Both are fertile soil in which Christian stewardship grows.

The first two chapters of Genesis are the basis for Creation spirituality. Do you know how important these first chapters of the Bible are to a Christian world view? I'm not just thinking of issues people make so much of these days, like the how of Creation (is it evolution or creationism?) or the when of

Creation Stewardship

Creation (Is the earth young or old?). I'm thinking of the Who of creation, that is God.
"In the beginning, God ..." Genesis begins. Creation starts with God. Christian spirituality starts with God. So does Christian stewardship.

But the writer of Genesis continues: "In the beginning, God created ..." Creation starts with God, but moves quickly to the material universe. The first of three emphases from Genesis 1 and 2 linking spirituality and stewardship is the meaning of matter.

Christian stewardship has a lot to do with material things, how we view them, and how we use them. Christian spirituality not only has to do with material things but also is about the invasion of the spiritual world into the tangible, material world. Christian spirituality, which is truly biblical, is earthed in the practical realities of everyday life, in the material things so important in life, and even in our physical bodies, which the New Testament tells us are "temples of the Holy Spirit" (1 Corinthians 6:19).

Genesis 1 and 2 is about that kind of earthly spirituality. God didn't just create invisible ideas or spirits you can't see or handle. God made things, matter, bodies, flesh and blood.

There are at least two false ways of seeing the material world. Genesis 1 and 2 combats them both. One view, prevalent in the ancient world, and even now, is that *creation is god*. Ancient peoples thought the divine and the creation were one.

Many modern people do the same. Pantheism, the idea that everything is god and god is everything, is an extremely popular view in contemporary America. Associated with pantheism is the popularity today of astrology, which suggests that our whole life is controlled by the stars. In other words, creation is god.

Spirituality in a Mixed-Up Age

But Genesis says, "No!" God is the Creator and not one in essence with His creation. Nature is the work of God's hand and is not God. Our destiny is in God's hand not the stars.

2. The other false view of the material world is that creation is bad. Anything material or physical has sometimes been regarded as evil or at least irrelevant. This thread of thinking running through the church's history has led people to think that sex, the body, food, sensual pleasure are all unimportant, if not absolutely evil. But Genesis 1 and 2 says, "No!" All God created is good, in fact, very good. We get the picture of God delighting in what He has made, reveling in His creation.

It is true that Genesis 3 follows Chapters 1 and 2. Genesis 3 provides a sobering story, whose impact we have felt ever since, a story about how sin has affected the whole creation. But Genesis 3 does not undo or nullify Genesis 1 and 2. The creation, including the human being, is still subject to the divine declaration of good, even very good.

But what's all this got to do with stewardship, with managing my money or taking up the offering at church? Let me observe some practical implications. For one thing *Creation spirituality relishes and celebrates the created world as a gift of God.* It savors taste, color, shape, feel, sound. In much of evangelical Christianity we fall short of wholeheartedly celebrating the Creation. I see a fear of enjoying even genuine and good pleasure too much. Creation spirituality relishes and celebrates the created world.

Furthermore, and here is the stewardship implication, *Creation spirituality moves me to give out of a glad and grateful response to the gift of God's creation.* Creation is God's good and wonderful gift to us. Creation spirituality moves me to respond to God's gift with a joyful generosity modeled by the Creator God.

194

Creation Stewardship

A Creation spirituality is thus not stingy, not limiting, not merely calculating, but glad, grateful and celebrative. Sometimes, when we talk about the principle of tithing, Christians will ask, "Well, should it be on gross or net income?" That's beside the point! Creation spirituality doesn't try to find ways to limit giving like we try to find ways to limit our taxes. Creation spirituality involves a glad, grateful and generous response to a gracious, generous and creative God.

There's a second emphasis linking stewardship and spirituality in Genesis 1 and 2. It has to do with the ownership of God. As Creator, God is owner. The One who makes is the One who owns.

The Old Testament recognized the ownership of God in the principle of the tithe. The Creator God owned what people had, owning even the land on which they lived and worked. Thus, they were to give back a tenth of the land's produce in recognition that He owned it all.

This theme of God's ownership is amplified in the Psalms, where we read that "The earth is the Lord's, ..." (Psalms 24:1) and that "the cattle on a thousand hills" belong to God (Psalms 50:10).

The theme of God's ownership is also reflected in Paul's teaching about Jesus as God's instrument of creation. Creation, wrote Paul, is "by him and for him" (Colossians 1:16). He is Creator and Owner.

Dutch theologian and statesman, Abraham Kuyper, once exclaimed that there is not a single square inch of the universe over which Christ does not say, "This is mine!" Do we believe that?

A dad tells of a little family travel ritual. When the family car would pass a hill covered with grazing cattle, Dad would say, "that's number 631," picking that or some other random

Spirituality in a Mixed-Up Age

number. "What do you mean, 631?" one of the children would respond. Dad's reply, "Oh, God has a thousand of those hills and all the cattle on them belong to Him. That one's just number 631 out of the thousand."

That's Creation spirituality. Here's the stewardship implication: *Creation spirituality moves me to give out of a heartfelt recognition that God owns it all anyway.* I give recognizing by such giving that He is the Owner of it all. The prophet Malachi went so far as to call nonpayment of the tithe "robbing God" (Malachi 3:8-9). Does that sound harsh? It makes good sense if we really believe God owns it all.

A third emphasis in Creation spirituality is *stewardship of human beings.* According to Genesis, human beings are created in the very image of God. What a high identity role!

Ancient Egyptians spoke of their pharaoh as "the image of God." The ancient Assyrians referred to their king as being "God's very image." Apparently, Genesis used a known idea to express an idea that was unknown at that time. Genesis gives all human beings a royal identity comparable to the ancient pharaoh, to a king or queen.

God gives all human beings royal obligations to go along with that royal identity and role. As humans, we are given dominion over the earth under God. However, we are not just to exercise power, but rather, we are to exercise it in the manner of our Creator God. We are not to be just rulers, but caretakers, stewards. How would God take care of the forest, the streams and oceans, the birds, animals and fish, my body, all the resources at my disposal?

Unfortunately, these days the idea of caring for the creation is often co-opted by the New Age movement, by people who don't believe in a uniquely Christian doctrine of Creation, by those who sometimes deify the earth, making it a goddess. A

Creation Stewardship

biblical spirituality, a Creation spirituality, teaches us that along with our exalted role of image-bearers of God comes this important responsibility of being caretakers of what God has made and what God owns.

This creation theme comes to a head in the great New Testament understanding of "steward," one who cares for and uses the resources of another. Jesus told stories about stewards, servants of a master, who were responsible for the use of the master's resources. In talking about the stewardship of the gospel, the Apostle Paul declares that we should regard ourselves as "stewards of the mysteries of God." "Moreover," Paul writes, "it is required of stewards that one be found faithful" (1 Corinthians 4:1-2).

Here's another stewardship implication: *Creation spirituality moves me to give because God has entrusted it to me.* Think of it: God lets us have a share in what He is doing. God gives me the privilege of managing some of His resources. God gives me the opportunity of using some of those resources to support what God is doing. Stewardship involves being co-workers with God.

When my wife's parents died, we faced the question of tithing money from her parents' estate. Instead of giving a tenth of it immediately, we decided to invest a tenth in an account whose proceeds every year would be dedicated for the support of God's work in some way. Soon after investing the money, we got a small dividend check, which we gave to our church's building fund, but I wondered why it wasn't more. I thought maybe this isn't going to be such a good deal for God. But upon checking toward the end of the year, I found that only a small portion of the proceeds from that investment was coming back to us, the rest being reinvested. At our request, all of the proceeds beyond the original investment, including capital

Spirituality in a Mixed-Up Age

gains and all dividends, were sent to us so we could give them away. And it turns out God did pretty well for Himself this past year!

It was exciting to be a vehicle through whom God could work. We are junior partners but yet real partners with God. As God blesses His account, we get to give it away. But really, that's what Christian giving is all about. As God blesses us, we give for the support of what God is doing in the world.

Good stewardship for Christians, then, depends not on intense appeals for money, not on guilt-producing emphases, not on manipulative devices to foster giving, but on biblical spirituality, a creation spirituality, which starts with God and responds to Who God is and what God has done. That kind of spirituality is rooted in Creation, in right thinking and appropriate living based on Creation.

27

Exodus Stewardship

That kind of spirituality is also rooted in the Exodus. In addition to a Genesis spirituality, there is an Exodus spirituality, which nurtures and nourishes Christian stewardship.

Exodus is the story of liberation, from Egyptian bondage. The Passover festival, which marks this liberation, has been celebrated by Hebrew people as a kind of Independence Day, a Jewish Fourth of July.

Christians understand the Exodus as a symbol of redemption in Jesus. As a consequence of our sin, all people have fallen into bondage, involving separation from God and from one another. But a Deliverer offers a way of salvation, a way out of bondage. This new Moses, this Jesus, offers a New Covenant, a new relationship with God. There is also set before us a promised land of life in Christ. Exodus spirituality responds to what God has done for us not just in Creation, but also in redemption, not only in making us, but in liberating us.

Four words capsulize the meaning of Exodus spirituality and have crucial implications for our thinking about Christian stewardship. The first word is *liberation*.

In the first Exodus, the people of God were liberated from oppressive bondage. So, too, in the Christian life, God's people today may experience liberation from bondage to legalism, to the enslaving power of sin, and to the grip of material

Spirituality in a Mixed-Up Age

things. Redemption spirituality is about liberation from any kind of bondage, including bondage to material things.

Material things are not evil in themselves, since God declared the material world He created good. Yet, even good things can enslave me if I lose perspective on them. Even good things can hold me in bondage if I forget that God is my ultimate priority, not some thing.

Have you noticed how material things can become a focus around which everything in our lives revolves? I once read of a traveler in a Third World country who went on a train trip. He settled into the public compartment, placing his suitcase in a rack above the bunk he was to occupy. Having been warned to keep an eye on his luggage at all times, the traveler tried to stay awake all night.

Close to morning, having struggled with sleep for hours, but having succeeded in keeping his luggage in view, he finally closed his eyes for a short while. He opened them with a start, glanced at his suitcase and saw that it was gone. "Thank God," he exclaimed, "now I can go to sleep!" Even good and appropriate things can so hold us in their grip that everything in life revolves around them.

Jesus talked about "mammon." "You cannot serve God and mammon" (Matthew 6:24). Most newer translations render the word mammon as "money." Originally, it was a word for material possession without any negative connotation. Mammon referred to wealth entrusted to someone for safekeeping, like something one puts in a bank safe-deposit box. But mammon came to mean that in which a person puts his or her trust, a kind of god. Do we see the progression from something one entrusts to someone to something in which one puts his or her trust? That's why Jesus said, "You cannot serve God and mammon."

Exodus spirituality is about liberation from and redemp-

Exodus Stewardship

tion from bondage to any power other than God. And a vital part of that liberation is learning how to give away. Nothing so effectively breaks the power material things can have over us than giving them away. Try it, you'll see!

Richard Foster, in his book *Money, Sex and Power*, has written: "The Christian is given the high calling of using mammon without serving mammon. We are using mammon when we allow God to determine our economic decisions. We are serving mammon when we allow mammon to determine our economic decisions. We simply must decide who is going to make our decisions — God or mammon."

A second word linking Exodus spirituality with Christian stewardship is *celebration*. For the Hebrew people, Passover became a gratitude-filled celebration of liberation from bondage. Every year, Hebrew families remembered the story of how God had delivered their people. There was the celebration meal, a family eating together in glad remembrance of liberation. Upon arrival in the promised land of Canaan, each head of household was to take some first fruits of the land in a basket to the worship center. This was to be offered to God with rejoicing and thanksgiving for God's goodness (Deuteronomy 26:1-4).

All God's people have reason for grateful celebration. We are all slaves redeemed from bondage. We affirm this every Sunday when we gather for worship in the shadow of the cross, remembering that it is because of what Jesus did for us on that cross that we are freed from slavery. We sing songs of praise for our redemption. We re-enact the sacred supper of the Lord, retelling what He did for us and how grateful we are for His gift of redemption. Many Christians call the Lord's Supper the "eucharist," which simply means "the thanksgiving."

When we come together for worship, we hear from Scripture the meaning of our liberation and how this redeemed

Spirituality in a Mixed-Up Age

life should be lived. We also bring our tithes and offerings for the support of God's work and for the meeting of human needs in God's name. Christians are people who gratefully celebrate our liberation.

Some Christians give money to God out of fear. One man tells of being raised on the theology that you give or "God gets you." As a 10-year-old, he recalls coming home from school to hear that the neighbor's house had burned to the ground. That night his mother said to the family around the dinner table, "Well, I knew something would happen. You know, Henry stopped tithing last year!"

Some Christians give to God merely out of legalism. They feel they have to give, and they do but are not happy about it. I love the story of a mother managing her fussy child in a worship service. After service, she explained to the pastor that her child was difficult to handle because he was teething.

"Your child didn't bother me" said the pastor. "But," he continued, "I did notice your husband. He seemed to be grinding his teeth a lot."

"Oh," said the woman, "he's not teething; he's just started tithing, and he's not happy about it!"

Christian stewardship based on an Exodus spirituality is not based merely on fear or on a teeth-grinding legalism, but in gratitude for what God has done in liberating us from Egypt.

When the Apostle Paul wrote to Corinthian Christians urging an offering for the especially poor Christians in Jerusalem, he advocated a celebration of gratitude in giving. "God loves a cheerful giver," was one thing Paul told them (2 Corinthians 9:7). The word translated "cheerful" is the same Greek word from which we get "hilarious." God loves hilarious givers! The apostle climaxes an extended segment of his second letter to the Corinthians devoted to this offering with the exclama-

Exodus Stewardship

tion, "Thanks be to God for His indescribable gift!" (2 Corinthians 9:15).

Beyond liberation and celebration, there is *discipleship*. Soon after they were liberated from Egyptian bondage, God gave the Hebrew people the law through Moses. Through this law God told them how people in covenant relationship with Him should live. Through this law God told them how to live in a holy and wholesome manner. Torah, which is how the Hebrews described the law, means "He points the finger." God's law pointed God's people in God's way.

The Torah acknowledged God's ownership in all things by providing for the tithe. Ten percent of the Hebrews' resources was dedicated to supporting the needs of the worship center and the needs of those who devoted their lives to the priesthood. This was simply the lifestyle of those redeemed and liberated people. This was the way people who celebrated their liberation lived.

Today, when Jesus calls men and women out of bondage, He calls them to follow Him, to not be just converts but His disciples. Being then a disciple of Jesus involves a lifestyle of obedience not just to the Law of Moses but to the lordship of Jesus. Being a disciple of Jesus means that we consciously, willingly, gladly submit to His lordship in our lives. "Jesus is Lord" means Jesus is Lord of my money.

Christian disciples are not required by law to give a tithe of their resources. We don't live under the law of Moses but under the grace of God expressed in Jesus. But if, under law, people gave 10 percent, the question we face is, *how can we who live under grace do less?*

A "stewardship testimony" one Sunday was given by a person who told of being converted to Christ out of the occult. Soon after accepting Christ, she found that Christians had this practice of tithing. Since she didn't know any better, as she put

Spirituality in a Mixed-Up Age

it, she just started tithing too. She understood that was just what Christians do. It was part of being a disciple of Jesus. In the 15 plus years since that time, she has tithed even in times when her relationship with God has been shaky, and she hasn't been sure of a lot of things. The practice of tithing has been a tangible link with God and a visible reminder of being a disciple of Jesus.

There's one more word which ties Exodus spirituality with Christian stewardship. It is *community*.

Out of the Exodus and through the wilderness wanderings of God's people, a nation was formed, a community. Exodus tells of God's purpose to make the Hebrew people "a holy nation, a kingdom of priests" (Exodus 19:5-6). They were to be a community of the redeemed.

Christian spirituality is always lived out in the context of belonging to the community. We experience God, and we live out the life of the Spirit within the community of believers. Christian stewardship also begins and continues in this community context. Our participation in community is expressed in our tangible, financial support for the needs of the community both locally and on a wider scale. We support our own local community of faith in its efforts to carry out Christian ministries in our community.

Though the local church may not present its needs in as sophisticated and gripping a manner as some other organizations today, its needs are just as great and worthy of support. We give money for world missions and for educational institutions. We support members of our community in cross-cultural and international service to the Lord. We may give money directly to individuals who are in need. These are extensions of the Christian community. This is the community of faith at work.

Exodus Stewardship

When the Apostle Paul promoted an offering for needy Christians in Jerusalem, it was the Christian community responding to the needs of its own. Christians in Corinth and in Macedonia were connected by common faith with the needy Christians in Jerusalem. A community must take care of its own (2 Corinthians 8 and 9).

Furthermore, according to Paul's model, it is the community that administers the stewardship of God's people. Paul gave detailed instructions about how the offering for Christians in Jerusalem was to be administered by the Corinthian church (1 Corinthians 16:1-4). The community was to handle the money consecrated for this purpose in an orderly, systematic and beyond-reproach manner.

Liberation, celebration, discipleship and community are all elements of an Exodus spirituality. They are a response to what God has done for us through the bondage-breaking power of the cross and the Spirit of Jesus in us. Integral to that kind of life is obedient, faithful and joyful giving to the work of God in the world.

Stewardship and spirituality *are* closely linked. Stewardship grows in the fruitful soil of a developing spiritual life. Thus, I invite us to review our attitudes toward money, to think again about how we use it and how we give it. Is our giving to God based on principle rather than on feelings and on how much we think we can afford? Is our giving regular and consistent, not spasmodic and occasional? Is our giving with joy?

Ben Gill, who has spent 25 years helping people, as he puts it, "learn the gift of giving," writes of one thing which has become increasingly clear to him. It is this: "The happiest people on earth are the people who have learned the joy of giving."[2]

Endnotes

Chapter 1
1. Charles Colson, "The Year of the Neo-Pagan," *Christianity Today* (March 6, 1995): 88.
2. *USA Today* (August 10, 1994): 1D.
3. *Life* (March, 1994): 54ff.
4. Michael Green and Paul Stevens, *New Testament Spirituality* (Guildford: Eagle, 1994), 3.
5. Kenneth Leech, *Soul Friend: An Invitation to Spiritual Direction* (San Francisco: Harper, 1992), 140ff.
6. Ibid., 143.
7. Ibid., 151.
8. Eugene Peterson, *Subversive Spirituality* (Vancouver: Regent College, 1994), 19.

Chapter 5
1. William Hadey and Janet Bermondi, *A Generation Alone* (Downers Grove: Intervarsity Press, 1994), 56.

Chapter 7
1. Robert Meye, "To Grace a Debtor," *Theology: News and Notes* (June 1993): 10.
2. Thomas Oden, *The Transforming Power of Grace* (Nashville: Abingdon, 1993), 15, 16.

Chapter 8
1. Bruce Shelley and Marshall Shelley, *Consumer Church* (Downers Grove: Intervarsity Press, 1992), 57.
2. Charles Colson, *The Body* (Word: Dallas, 1992), 73.
3. Peterson, *Subversive Spirituality*, 22.
4. Bruce Milne, *We Belong Together* (Downers Grove: Intervarsity Press, 1978), 19.
5. John Stott, *God's New Society* (Downers Grove: Intervarsity Press, 1979), 172.

Chapter 9
1. Mike Bellah, *Baby Boom Believers* (Wheaton: Tyndale House, 1988), 131.
2. J.I. Packer, *Knowing God* (Downers Grove: Intervarsity Press, 1973), 21.

Spirituality in a Mixed-Up Age

3. Arden K. Barden, quoted in *Christianity Today* (January 15, 1988): 35.
4. David Hansen, *The Art of Pastoring* (Downers Grove: Intervarsity Press, 1994), 104.

Chapter 11
1. M. Scott Peck, *The Road Less Traveled* (New York: Simon and Schuster, 1978), 15.

Chapter 12
1. J.B. Phillips, *Plain Christianity* (New York: McMillan, 1954), 70.

Chapter 13
1. Henri Nouwen, *Here and Now* (New York: Crossroad, 1994), 135.
2. F.F. Bruce, quoted in *Romans*, Tyndale New Testament Commentaries (Grand Rapids: Eerdmans, 1963), 166.
3. Maxie Dunnam, *The Christian Way* (Grand Rapids: Zondervan, 1987), 66.
4. Edward Sugden, *Ed Wesley's Standard Sermons* (London: Epworth Press, 1966), 1:209.

Chapter 14
1. Robert Mulholland, quoted in *Invitation to Journey* (Downers Grove: Intervarsity Press, 1993), 20.

CHAPTER 17
1. Frederick Buechner, *Whistling in the Dark* (San Francisco: Harper and Row, 1988), 103.
2 Ibid., 104.

CHAPTER 18
1. Alister McGrath, *Spirituality in an Age of Change* (Grand Rapids: Zondervan, 1994), 28.
2. Ibid., 47.
3. Ibid., 190.

CHAPTER 19
1. Henri Nouwen, *Life Signs* (New York: Doubleday, 1960), 68

CHAPTER 20
1. Charles Spurgeon, *Faith's Checkbook* (Chicago: Moody Press, 1987), 5.

CHAPTER 21
1. C.S. Lewis, *Mere Christianity* (New York: McMillan, 1960), 155.
2. McGrath, *Spirituality in an Age of Change*, 80.

CHAPTER 26
1. *Leadership* (Spring 1981): 105.

CHAPTER 27
1. Richard Foster, *Money, Sex and Power* (San Francisco: Harper and Row, 1985), 56.
2. Ben Gill, *The Joy of Giving* (Dallas: Myriad Communications, 1994), 2.